THE EAST COAST
BED &
BREAKFAST
GUIDE

The Shire Inn, Chelsea, Vermont

NEW ENGLAND AND THE MID-ATLANTIC

Bed & Breakfast Guide

EAST COAST

BY ROBERTA GARDNER, NAOMI BLACK, AND TERRY BERGER

Photographs by George W. Gardner

DESIGNED AND PRODUCED BY ROBERT R. REID
AND TERRY BERGER

PRENTICE HALL PRESS

NEW YORK

FRONTISPIECE PHOTOGRAPH:
Staircase detail from the house at Logan Circle, Washington, D.C.

COUNTRY SPREAD:
Amish farmer en route to market near Intercourse, Pennsylvania.

Editorial assistance by Michele Sensale.
Map by Anthony St. Aubyn.
Photographs on pages 106 and 107 by Will Faller.
Photograph on page 105 courtesy of the Manor House.
Photograph at bottom of page 104 by Susan Cragin.

Published by Prentice Hall Press
A Division of Simon & Schuster, Inc.
Gulf + Western Building
One Gulf + Western Plaza
New York, New York 10023

———————————————————

A Robert Reid/Terry Berger production
Typeset in Bodoni Book by Monotype Composition Company, Baltimore.
Printed and bound by Mandarin Offset Marketing (H.K.) Ltd., Hong Kong.

1 2 3 4 5 6 7 8 9 10

Library of Congress Cataloging-in-Publication Data

Gardner, Roberta Homan.
   The East Coast bed & breakfast guide.

   1. Bed and breakfast accommodations—New England—
Directories. 2. Bed and breakfast accommodations—Middle
Atlantic States—Directories. I. Black, Naomi. II. Berger,
Terry. III. Gardner, George William, 1940–   . IV. Title.
V. Title: East Coast bed and breakfast guide. VI. Title: Bed
& breakfast guide. VII. Title: Bed and breakfast guide.
TX907.G33   1986   647'.9474   86-18644

ISBN   0-671-62947-6

CONTENTS

Bed & Breakfast in the City

Bed & Breakfast in the Country

NOTE

Readers should note that the information within these pages is as accurate as can be at press time. Rates and amenities do change, however, so every effort should be made to call the bed and breakfasts in advance. The following notes will help in making reservations:

• Rates are for the room. Unless noted, there is no difference for single or double occupancy.

• Many bed and breakfasts now require a two-night minimum stay on weekends.

• Be prepared to pay anywhere from ten percent to a full night's stay in advance as a deposit. Some B & Bs have even stricter rules. After making a telephone reservation, be sure you follow up with a payment or your reservation will be forfeited. Also, be aware that many places also have a minimal cancellation fee.

• Let your hosts know if you have any allergies. It is best not to be surprised on arrival.

• The recent rise in insurance rates has affected inns considerably, so do not be surprised at changes taking place since publication of this book.

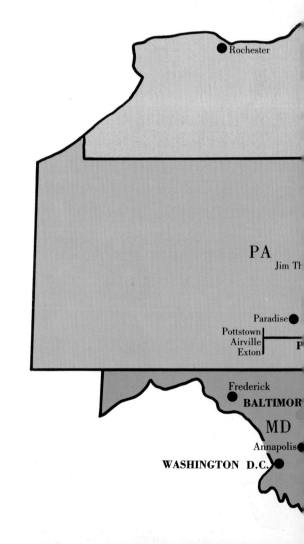

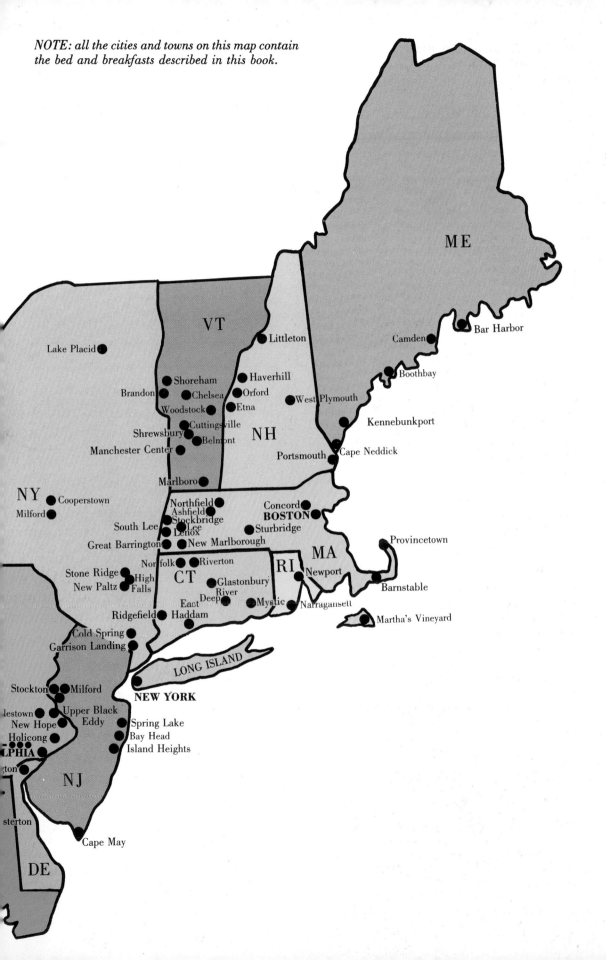

NOTE: *all the cities and towns on this map contain the bed and breakfasts described in this book.*

ME

VT

Lake Placid

Littleton

Camden

Bar Harbor

Shoreham

Haverhill

Boothbay

Brandon

Chelsea

Orford

Woodstock

Etna

West Plymouth

Cuttingsville

Kennebunkport

Shrewsbury

Belmont

NH

Manchester Center

Portsmouth

Cape Neddick

Marlboro

NY

Cooperstown

Northfield

Concord

Milford

Ashfield

BOSTON

Stockbridge

South Lee

Lee

Sturbridge

Lenox

Great Barrington

New Marlborough

Provincetown

Norfolk

Riverton

RI

MA

Stone Ridge

High

CT

Newport

New Paltz

Falls

Glastonbury

River

Barnstable

East

Deep

Ridgefield

Haddam

Mystic

Narragansett

Cold Spring

Martha's Vineyard

Garrison Landing

LONG ISLAND

Stockton

Milford

NEW YORK

lestown

Upper Black

Spring Lake

New Hope

Eddy

Bay Head

Holicong

Island Heights

LPHIA

ton

NJ

sterton

Cape May

DE

BED & BREAKFAST
IN THE CITY

BOSTON

Left, the reception hall. Above, a private sun porch off the bedroom.

NORTH SHORE

A family home

Set on a fourteen acre estate, this rambling brown-shingled twenty-two room "cottage" is close to the fishing boats of Gloucester and the sailboat fleets of Manchester and scenic Rockport. There are acres of woodsy terrain to explore. It has its own tennis court, it is accessible to riding stables, and is a ten-minute walk from the beach.

Expansive and multi-leveled, the house is homey and casual. Old wood floors, comfortable plush period pieces, eyelit curtains, and large fireplaces abound. A sense of family history prevails: toys belonging to the father of the hostess, the host's father's art school diploma, over a hundred years old, passed down furniture and books, a large framed photo of the original Princeton Tiger belonging to the hostess's father (Princeton 1906).

Guests, essentially, have the run of the house.

Fires are always laid, ready to be lit, and a continental breakfast will be brought to the room upon request. A full breakfast is served near the fireplace in the ample dining room and, when weather permits, on the closed-in porch where wicker furniture overlooks the grounds.

Both guest rooms have old white iron bedsteads covered with delicate antique quilts. One room has an English charcoal grate fireplace and screened-in private deck overlooking a stand of hemlocks. The other chamber has a floral painted chest, oak desk, rag rug, and an antique white iron crib, in addition to two twin beds.

Framed on a wall a homily proclaims: "Mental health is our greatest wealth". The beauty of nature, an abiding sense of tranquility, sweet air, and the bliss of solitude here are all contributing factors.

NORTH SHORE. Twenty-two room Victorian estate on fourteen wooded acres. Open year-round. Two guest rooms each with private bath. Rates: $55 and $65 a room. Children welcome; pets welcome; no smoking; MasterCard/Visa/American Express. Close to Gloucester and Salem. Forty minutes to Boston. *Represented by Bed and Breakfast Associates, Bay Colony Ltd., Boston, MA.*

A beehive fireplace, original to the oldest part of the house.

MEDFORD

An 18th-century architectural jewel

Seven miles from the center of Boston, this large, eighteenth-century home is an architectural gem. The original section of the house was built circa 1720, and detailing, such as two-panel doors, vertical plank walls with hair plaster, and original hand-wrought hardware, remains intact. By 1799 the house changed hands, and its wealthy new owner undertook a major renovation in the Federal style. A few of the fine details reflecting that period are twelve-over-twelve window sashes with a number of original, Crown glass panes, spackle-painted floors, and fine mantels and doors. The breakfast room—a contemporary addition—opens onto a slate patio and formal gardens that guests enjoy during warm months of the year.

MEDFORD . Eighteenth-century home that retains its original beehive hearth. Open year-round. Two guest rooms, shared bath. Rates: $50 single, $55 double. Continental breakfast. No pets; no smoking. In residential neighborhood, close to Tufts University and 15 minutes from downtown Boston. *Represented by Bed and Breakfast Associates, Bay Colony Ltd., Boston, MA.*

CHESTNUT HILL

Children welcome

Here is an unusual find: a family home complete with four children and anxious for more. Guests are welcome and comfortable here with their children in a home whose antiques the hostess claims are child-proof. Next to a den-type guest room, there is a playroom in the basement, complete with hobby horse, easel, jigsaw puzzles, gym mat, record player, and musical instruments. There are swings, a sandbox, and kiddie pool outside.

Interesting furnishings pop up here and there; two Jacobean chairs covered with needlepoint cushions, hand woven Spanish rugs, an ornate Empire mirror, an elegant wood-burning stove. Ancestors of both host and hostess vie for attention: portraits and photographs of weddings, babies, homes, and by-gone days. Dominating the dining room is a grand portrait of the host's great grandfather, a Pittsburgh banker. Here the hostess serves up pancakes, muffins, and jams laced with blueberries, her specialty, in addition to homemade breads, cold cereals, and hot breakfast on request.

An expansive wrap around deck invites breakfasting and sunning amidst stately oaks and an occasional pheasant. The area has many fine jogging trails and is close to private schools, fine medical facilities, and Boston.

CHESTNUT HILL. Large older home with deck, located in quiet residential setting on two private acres. Open year-round. Three guest rooms with private and shared baths. Rates: $30-$65 double. Breakfast to suit included. Children welcome; no pets; smoking permitted; Visa/MasterCard/American Express. Near hospital area; five miles to Boston. *Represented by Bed and Breakfast Associates, Bay Colony Ltd., Boston, MA.*

BACK BAY

A brick townhouse on a restored street

The Back Bay of Boston is home to this 1881 bow-front brick townhouse on one of the beautifully restored streets of the St. Botolph area. Owned by a vivacious, outgoing professional couple, the townhouse enjoys special architectural features that include brownstone steps and exquisite stained-glass windows. From this vantage point, Symphony Hall, Copley Plaza, and the Prudential Center are an easy walk.

BACK BAY . Brick bow-front, 1881 brownstone. Open year-round. Two guest rooms, shared bath. Rates: $40 to $50 single, $55 to $60 double; $10 for third person. No children under ten; no pets; no smoking. In St. Botolph neighborhood, within walking distance of downtown Boston. *Represented by Bed and Breakfast Associates, Bay Colony, Ltd., Boston, MA.*

Living room, above, and the sunlit breakfast room, right.

The light-bejeweled entryway.

BACK BAY

A penthouse near Boston Common

Two blocks from the Boston Common and the charming swan boats of the Public Garden, and likewise close to the boutiques and shops lining Newbury Street, this fourth-floor Back Bay penthouse apartment is blessed with well-proportioned rooms lit by a skylight, and a spacious roof deck. Here, guests may while away the time soaking in the morning sun with a mug of bracing coffee or tea, or enjoying an impromptu picnic lunch overlooking the historic rooftops of Boston.

BACK BAY . Brownstone built in 1878, with fourth-floor, walk-up penthouse. Open year-round, except for occasional vacations. One guest room, private bath close by. Rates: $55 single, $60 double. Continental breakfast. No facilities for infants; no pets; no smoking. In the heart of Boston, 2 blocks from Boston Common. *Represented by Bed and Breakfast Associates, Bay Colony Ltd., Boston, MA.*

NEW YORK

GREENWHICH VILLAGE

Sophisticated décor

In addition to a panoramic view of Lobro, the newly developed part of lower Broadway, this heart-of-the-village bed and breakfast is a fifteen minute jaunt to Chinatown and less than that to Little Italy and the lower east side. Bordering on Soho and its art galleries, boutiques, wearable art, and exciting new restaurants, the bed and breakfast is a stone's throw away from bakery/ cafés serving such fare as sfogliatella, napoleons, and pignoli tarts.

The airy cheerful apartment has two guestrooms: a pretty floral bedroom/sitting room with Eastlake chest and mirror, where you can sit up in bed and survey Bleecker Street, and a den with highriser, shelves of books, a desk, and typewriter. Art work covers all the walls—movie posters, two surprisingly striking vintage Red Cross posters, botanicals. A varied selection of greenery and a colorfully patterned rug add to the charm and warmth.

The hosts are so well liked that guests have been known to throw parties for them before leaving for home. An entry in the guest book reads: "I have a new home in a big city. I will never be lonely again."

GREENWICH VILLAGE. Modern high rise building with views of lower Broadway. Open year-round. Two guest rooms, with a shared bath. Rates: $65 single, $80 double. Continental breakfast included. Children over six welcome; no pets; smoking permitted; MasterCard/Visa/American Express. Close to Chinatown, Little Italy, Washington Square Park, Soho. Two toy poodles in residence. *Represented by Urban Ventures, Inc., New York City.*

UPPER WEST SIDE

Cooking classes on Wednesday nights

If you arrive on a Wednesday night, you might partake of one of Wendy Berry's cooking classes which convene in her tiny apartment kitchen. A caterer and photographer, Wendy also works for New York's Board of Education. Her two-level apartment in a large and elegant brownstone is located on a tree-lined street on the Upper West Side. Just a block from Columbus Avenue, the neighborhood is fast becoming a haven for young professionals. This influx of the upwardly mobile has triggered a renaissance; the Upper West Side has blossomed into the most dynamic neighborhood in all of Manhattan. Every day new restaurants, fabulous food emporiums, and trendy boutiques appear, replacing the down-at-the-heels businesses that characterized the Columbus Avenue of yesterday.

UPPER WEST SIDE. Two-level apartment in brownstone townhouse. Open year-round. One guest room, shared bath. Rates: $55 single, $70 double. Continental breakfast. No children under twelve; no pets; no smoking. In Upper West Side neighborhood with endless possibilities for entertainment. Represented by *The B & B Group (New Yorkers at Home) Inc., NYC.*

UNITED NATIONS

An international neighborhood

Within view of the Chrysler Building and the United Nations, this snug little studio apartment is available for weekends. Modest but neat, its bulls-eye mirror and Hepplewhite chest add charm. Located in one of Manhattan's safest neighborhoods where U.N. diplomats enjoy extra police protection, it has its own round-the-clock doorman.

Although equipped with a working kitchen, the apartment does not entertain many "eaters-in." Guests are easily wooed by enticing alternatives. The neighborhood is a hot bed of New York's oldest and best loved restaurants: The Palm, Christ Cella, Peng's, Lutece, Smith & Wolensky. . . . The hostess has devised a list to explain and simplify the choices.

Guests may board a convenient crosstown bus to Manhattan's theater district or to Lincoln Center.

UNITED NATIONS. Studio apartment in historic building between the United Nations and the Chrysler Building. Open year-round. Bath and kitchenette. Available for weekends. Rates: $75 a night for one or two persons. No children; no pets; no smoking. *Represented by The B & B Group (New Yorkers at Home) Inc., NYC.*

GRAMERCY PARK

Historical comfort

Between Gramercy and Stuyvesant Parks, in an old landmark building that traces its history back to Peter Stuyvesant, this triplex bed and breakfast is pure delight. The streets surrounding it have been well walked by the famous figures who have lived here, such as Mark Twain, O. Henry, Anton Dvorak, and Samuel Tilden.

Shaded and draped in paisley, the oak floored parlor has sofas piled high with Persian printed pillows. A Victorian china cupboard, drop leaf desk, silver tea service, and an old railroad clock add interest and warmth. Breakfast is served at a round oak table under a floral crystal drop chandelier.

Whether you are nestled in the bright Mexican-yellow room with pink accents on the lowest level or two flights up in the space with skylighted gallery and access to the geranium-potted deck, you will be pleased with your surroundings.

The hostess, who is native to Manhattan, will knowledgably direct you, depending upon your interests. There is a constant blossoming of trendy restaurants in this newly energized area as well as the old standbys like Pete's Tavern, Sal Anthony's, Fat Tuesdays, and the Gramercy Park Hotel.

GRAMERCY PARK. Landmark brownstone building. Open year-round. Two guest rooms with shared bath. Rates: $65 single, $80 double. Expanded continental breakfast included. Children welcome; no pets; smoking permitted; MasterCard/Visa/American Express. Near to Gramercy Park, Greenwich Village, Soho, midtown. *Represented by Urban Ventures, Inc., New York City.*

MURRAY HILL

Manhattan's quintessential bed and breakfast

The hostess, a designer of women's clothing, has used the color, style, and decoration elements of her trade, as fine tools. She has transformed three floors of a Murray Hill converted factory building into Manhattan's quintessential bed and breakfast.

Each of the floors has its own living room, dining room, kitchen, and laundry. Ten guest rooms with private and shared baths, sleep from one to four people. Ash, peach, honey, and cream hues combine in guest rooms and public spaces. A French display armoire, Oriental carpets, a vintage Japanese screen, and canvas-covered couches are set off by a profusion of healthy greenery. A variety of window exposures frame building tops of Manhattan's famous skyline: Art Deco details, water towers, cartouches that can be glimpsed at dawn's, dusk's, and midnight's revolving light.

The feeling here resembles a European pension. Although the ambiance is casual, guests respect each others privacy. With the freedom to do laundry and to use a country-style kitchen complete with a supply of liquor administered on the honor system, people feel relaxed enough to walk around in their robes. Guests easily come and go, keeping business appointments, sightseeing, discovering New York. Antiques dealers, artists, stock brokers, writers, designers, buyers—Americans and Europeans—find their way here.

Presided over by a beautiful and highly capable hostess, this is a true bed and breakfast in the grand tradition.

MURRAY HILL. Recently converted office building with splendid views of Manhattan building tops. Open year-round. Ten guest rooms, most with private baths. Rates: $75 double, $88 triple. Children welcome; no pets; smoking permitted; MasterCard/Visa/ American Express. Laundry and kitchen facilities. *Represented by Urban Ventures, Inc., New York City.*

A view of the East River

In addition to your own writing desk, VCR, and interesting assortment of books, there is a six-teenth floor terrace and a view of the East River from this upper East side apartment. It is comfortably appointed with Oriental carpets, plush couches, and French Provincial furniture. The hostess, a teacher at Phoenix House, a drug rehab center, is warm and welcoming.

Very conveniently located, this apartment is within walking distance of Gracie Mansion (Mayor Koch's Bed & Breakfast) and the 92nd Street Y, known for its cultural events. There are many interesting little restaurants in the neighborhood including Elaine's, the gathering place for the literati, and Paradise Pizza Café, the winner of a New York Pizza Taste-Off.

YORKVILLE. High rise building with doorman. Open year-round. One guest room or possibly entire apartment. Private bath. Rates: $55 single, $70 double. Continental breakfast included. No children; no pets; smoking permitted. *Represented by The B & B Group (New Yorkers at Home) Inc., NYC.*

Brownstone peace and tranquillity, above. An exotic breakfast setting, right.

Spacious brownstone in a dynamic area

A sense of spaciousness comes from the fact that this three-story brownstone townhouse is a single-family dwelling. The third floor guest rooms were once the children's bedrooms and retain souvenirs of their adolescence. Just off Columbus Avenue—the most up and coming neighborhood in Manhattan—guests are close to Central Park, the American Museum of Natural History, and Lincoln Center as well as a plethora of fascinating shops and wonderful restaurants.

UPPER WEST SIDE . Brownstone and brick townhouse, built in 1887, with goldfish pond in back yard. Open mid-September through May (closed during Christmas). Three guest rooms, shared bath. Rates: $44 single, $54 double. Continental breakfast. No children under twelve, no pets; smoking discouraged. Close to Lincoln Center and Columbus Avenue. *Represented by Urban Ventures, Inc., New York City.*

EAST HAMPTON

Private decks and modern luxury

East Hampton is a colonial town complete with village green, windmill , and a three-century-old cemetery. Surrounded by gently rolling hills, the area is conducive to quiet activities: walks on the beach, candlelight dinners, reading.

This contemporary cottage is nestled in the treetops, along a quiet lane just outside of town. Its natural siding blends with the landscape, and each room has a private deck and entrance of its own. With the perfect home from which to start the business, these hosts operate the bed and breakfast reservation service, Alternate Lodgings.

EAST HAMPTON . Contemporary home with floor-to-ceiling windows in the living room and a treetop deck. Open April through October. Three guest rooms, private and shared baths. Rates: $65 to $80 double. Continental breakfast daily, often full breakfast on Sunday. No children; no pets; Visa/MasterCard/American Express. *Represented by Alternate Lodgings, Inc., East Hampton, NY.*

Each luxurious guest room has a private entrance.

SOUTHAMPTON

A beach cottage, smart pubs, discos

The elegant summer cottages that line the beach at Southampton bespeak the days when this was mecca for the very wealthy. Though socialites are still in evidence, young professionals and jet-setters are giving new energy to the town. Home of Job's Lane, the Hampton's most prestigious shopping district, Southampton also nurtures a thriving social life and by night, comes alive with pubs and discos.

Outside of town, this secluded beach house has a sauna, a private beach with dock, and a wraparound deck with views of the water.

SOUTHAMPTON . Contemporary home in wooded setting, over-looking the ocean. Open year-round. Two guest rooms (with twins), shared. Rates: $70 double. Continental breakfast. No children; no pets. Sauna and private non-swimming beach with dock. *Represented by Alternate Lodgings, Inc., East Hampton, NY.*

Modern luxury and an ocean view.

Casual elegance on chic Long Island.

AMAGANSETT

Bluejeans and tennis shoes

"If I were asked what to pack for a stay in Amagansett, I would suggest blue jeans and tennis shoes," observes a life-long resident of the area. An artists' enclave for many years, this is one of the quietest of the Hampton's beach communities, though several of the beautiful town beaches do attract a singles crowd.

Along a sandy lane, walking distance to the beach, this home is the casually elegant, year-round residence of two New York City professionals.

AMAGANSETT . New England-style colonial home with private beach. Open year-round. One guest room, private bath. Rates $65 double. Continental or full breakfast available. No children; no pets; smoking discouraged. Within walking distance of the ocean; summer stock, fishing, sailing, excellent dining nearby. *Represented by Alternate Lodgings, Inc., East Hampton, NY.*

PHILADELPHIA

VALLEY FORGE

Well before George Washington

This large stone colonial is an ageless beauty of the pre-Revolutionary period. Nestled on four acres of magnificently wooded land, its title deeds can be traced back to William Penn in 1681.

The original part of the house was built before 1720. Two additions built later create the overall traditional colonial appearance. The last addition was completed in 1791.

Over the years, interior walls have been added and removed, but the original random width plank flooring, with hand-forged nails, remains. The old wood floors, fireplaces, stone walls, and stone smoke house were there when George Washington was at Valley Forge.

A highlight of a stay here is the full English-style breakfast, gracious served in the old part of the house in front of the colonial fireplace with a huge mantel and eight-foot-wide hearth.

Two guest rooms occupy the entire third floor, providing spacious privacy for couples or families. The rose and grey room has a canopied queen-sized bed. The second chamber exudes a fresh "peaches and cream" Victorian look and has an antique double brass bed and a twin bed.

VALLEY FORGE. Open year-round. Two guest rooms, each with a private bath. Rates: $45 single, $55 double. Hearty full breakfast included. Children welcome; cradle and crib available; guest refrigerator provided; pool in back yard. Five minutes to Valley Forge Park, one-half hour to Philadelphia. *Represented by Bed & Breakfast of Philadelphia, Philadelphia, PA.*

Left, the oldest part of the house

RITTENHOUSE SQUARE

Fashionable row house

The vivacious hosts of this sophisticated, gracious row house in ever-fashionable Rittenhouse Square have captured the casual elegance of revitalized Philadelphia. Their backgrounds in the arts and nonprofit corporations account for the melange of art visible throughout the house. Eclecticism reigns here, whether in the tasteful bedrooms, on the quiet flagstone patio, or in the high-ceilinged living room.

RITTENHOUSE SQUARE. circa 1860 row house on the National Register. Closed January, February, July, and August. Three guest rooms; private baths. Rates: $60, with $5 surcharge for stays of only one night. Full breakfast. Children over 16 welcome; no pets; smoking in the garden only. Close to the Philadelphia Art Museum, restaurants. *Represented by Bed & Breakfast of Philadelphia, Philadelphia, PA.*

Left, your sitting room, dogs not included, and one of two bedrooms, above.

CHESTER COUNTY

A gristmill in foxhunting country

One of the most atmospheric landscapes in the mid-Atlantic, the rolling hills of the Brandywine Valley are interspersed with charming stone houses and covered bridges. This rustic gristmill, built around 1750, has been converted into spacious living quarters, complete with first-floor stables that house the owner's two horses. Besides enjoying the gentle beauty of Chester County, guests may follow fox hunts, for which the area is famous.

CHESTER COUNTY . Eighteenth-century gristmill converted into a residence in 1946. Open year-round. Two guest rooms, shared bath. Rates: $45 single, $55 double. Full breakfast. Pets accepted; can accommodate 2 horses in winter, 4 in summer. Forty minutes from Pennsylvania Dutch country; weekly fox hunts; Longwood Gardens, Winterthur Museum nearby. *Represented by Bed and Breakfast of Philadelphia, Philadelphia, PA.*

Room in which to spread out and relax

A grandly proportioned Queen Anne-style townhouse, this bed and breakfast home gives guests room to spread out and really relax. The bedroom is large enough to easily handle two couches, two chairs, and a double bed and still leave lots of floor space. A television, radio, and a working fireplace, flanked by built-in bookcases, complete the room. One especially thoughtful touch is the electric coffeepot, filled and ready to go, just outside the door.

UNIVERSITY CITY . Queen Anne Victorian townhouse. Open year-round. One guest room, shared bath. Rates: $40 single, $50 double. Hearty continental breakfast served daily, full breakfast available on weekends. No pets. Near Civic Center; all of Philadelphia easily accessible. *Represented by Bed & Breakfast of Philadelphia, Philadelphia, PA.*

An original Eames chair in the guest room.

Entry hall to the spacious rooms.

Federal townhouse near Society Hill

Poised between Society Hill and NewMarket, visitors to the newly restored areas of "historic Philadelphia" couldn't ask for a more convenient location. Meticulously renovated, this 1811 Federal townhouse beautifully weds mellow woodwork, exposed beams and brickwork, a pine floor, and working fireplaces with contemporary furnishings. The popular NewMarket shopping and dining complex is visible through the French doors in the guest bedroom.

NEWMARKET . Federal-style home built in 1811, with contemporary décor. Open year-round. Two guest rooms, shared bath. Rates: $40 single, $50 double. Hearty continental breakfast; guests may prepare full breakfast if they wish. No children; no pets. In NewMarket area, within walking distance of the historic district. *Represented by Bed & Breakfast of Philadelphia, Philadelphia, PA.*

SPRING GARDEN

Near the Museum of Art

The owner of this home is a dedicated collector of American antiques. His century-old townhouse, just six blocks from the Philadelphia Museum of Art, contains a fine collection of museum-quality artifacts. The first-floor living room displays such treasures as a Shaker child's chair, a Pennsylvania farm bench with original decorative paint, and Hudson River School paintings. Bedrooms are decorated with pre-Revolutionary pewter, jacquard coverlets and Sabbath Day Lake four-slat rockers.

SPRING GARDEN . Simple townhouse built in 1856 and largely furnished with American antiques. Open year-round. Two guest rooms, shared bath. Rates: $35 single, $45 double. Full breakfast (prepared by guests during the week). No children; no pets. In Spring Garden district, near museums and Fairmount Park. *Represented by Bed & Breakfast of Philadelphia, Philadelphia, PA.*

Roughing it, Philadelphia style.

NORTH PHILADELPHIA

A back-garden greenhouse becomes a fantasy cottage

Decorated with a light and casual hand, this combination greenhouse-and-potting-shed cottage is so inviting that many guests simply disappear for days on end, succumbing to the intimacy of the setting. The cottage shares a broad expanse of lawn with the main house and is bordered on one side by a picturesque grape arbor, and on the other by a large swimming pool. Only twenty-five minutes from Center City, this fantasy cottage is an ideal romantic getaway.

NORTH PHILADELPHIA . Private cottage, a combination greenhouse and potting shed, on three acres. Open year-round. One guest room (the potting shed), private bath (greenhouse). Rates: $75 one or two people. Continental breakfast can be fixed from ample supplies in refrigerator. No facilities for young children; inquire about pets. Swimming pool on premises; stable, tennis, golf nearby. *Represented by Bed & Breakfast of Philadelphia, Philadelphia, PA.*

An antiques collection on permanent display.

BALTIMORE

SOCIETY· HILL GOVERNMENT HOUSE

Baltimore's official bed and breakfast

These adjoining historic townhouses have been completely renovated and refurbished into Baltimore's premier bed and breakfast establishment. The project was the brainchild of the dynamic mayor, William Donald Schaefer. Painstakingly researched for historical accuracy, the complex was worked on for three years before it could offer hospitality in the style and manner for which Baltimore is noted. Swathed in Bradbury and Bradbury wallpaper, bedecked in Scalamandré and Schumacher fabrics, and outfitted with both antiques and fine reproductions, this grande dame has never appeared more glamorous.

The décor of the guest rooms, clearly influenced by the Federal period, reflects a traditional Baltimore style. Sitting areas in guest rooms offer a table and desk and TV. Guests choose from one of two continental breakfasts brought to their room at a specified time.

In addition to providing hospitality to bed and breakfast guests, the house often hosts official government functions in the splendid library, reception hall, and dining room. His Honor, the mayor, maintains an elegant suite for accommodating dignitaries, such as the Mayor of Rotterdam.

Another function performed here is the training of small groups of unemployed area citizens as housekeepers, bartenders, hostesses, and waiters to satisfy Baltimore's burgeoning need for hospitality services.

Historically correct and graciously managed, the Society Hill Government House is a premier bed and breakfast serving Baltimore and the greater community—yet another jewel in Baltimore's crown.

SOCIETY HILL GOVERNMENT HOUSE, 1125-1129 N. Calvert Street, Baltimore, MD 21202; (301) 752-7722; Judith Campbell and Deborah Fischer, innkeepers. Open year-round. Eighteen guest rooms, all with private bath and individual heating and cooling systems. Rates: $85–$105. Continental breakfast included. Children welcome; some pets (please call); smoking permitted; major credit cards accepted.

DIRECTIONS: call for directions.

Left, the entrance hall. Above, an opulent guest room.

ROLAND PARK

A fine collection of Northwest Indian art

A twenty-minute walk from Johns Hopkins University, this solid and elegant home is owned by a professor of medicine at the university, and his wife, a registered nurse with an interest in theater and the arts. While living in the Northwest, they acquired a fine collection of Northwest Indian art, which is displayed throughout the house. The impeccably clean guest room contains such amenities as a rocking chair, desk, attached bath, and a full dressing mirror.

ROLAND PARK. Colonial house with Federal embellishments. Open year-round. One guest room, private bath. Rates $45 single, $60 double. Full breakfast available. No smoking. Twenty-minute walk to Johns Hopkins University. *Represented by The Bed & Breakfast League, Ltd., Washington, DC.*

Entrance hall, showing an English brass rubbing on the landing.

BOLTON HILL

Light-filled guest rooms

Bolton Hill is a gracious urban neighborhood comprised of age-softened brick townhouses and tall shade trees. Just ten blocks from the Inner Harbor and close to Meyerhoff Symphony Hall, Lyric Theater, and the Baltimore Opera, this four-story rowhouse reflects the quiet good taste of its owner. Light-filled guest rooms on the top floor are spacious and comfortable. Guests may use the deck and private courtyard at the rear of the house.

BOLTON HILL . Four-story, turn-of-the-century townhouse. Open year-round. Two guest rooms, with private baths. Rates $55 per room. Hearty continental breakfast. No pets. On Bolton Hill, within walking district of Meyerhoff Symphony Hall and Lyric Theater. *Represented by The Bed & Breakfast League Ltd., Washington, DC; The Traveller in Maryland, Annapolis, MD.*

The richness and warmth of the parlor.

SOCIETY HILL HOPKINS

Four periods to choose from

The first room you notice is the charming parlor with its floral couch and matching wallpaper border, faux-finish mantel, etched glass Victorian chandelier, handsome artworks, and lace panel curtains. Guests often relax here with a cup of coffee or a glass of sherry.

The twenty-six guest rooms in this Spanish revival building have been arranged into four different periods: Federal, Victorian, Art Deco, and Contemporary. Guests are invited to reserve that period room that suits their mood or sense of fantasy.

Gray, lavender, peach, and blue offset the patterned rugs in the Federal room. The wallpaper border is a classical Adams frieze, and the mahogany armoire, Chippendale - style chairs, draped valances, and old prints enhance the period effect.

The Victorian room features a dressing mirror, wicker desk, white iron sweetheart bedstead, marble-topped tables, and lace curtains, while the Art Deco room has black lacquer furniture, Chinese-style lamps, twenties prints, and touches of period maroons and greys.

Finally, the contemporary room in browns and persimmon, accented in green, has a bed with brass headboard, rattan night stands, a pine armoire, and Hitchcock-style chair.

The monotony of the usual assemblage of small hotel rooms will not be found here; appointments do not smack of the decorator's art. Instead the charm of European bed and breakfasts and the warm hospitality of American country inns combines in a uniquely exciting blend.

SOCIETY HILL HOPKINS, 3404 St. Paul Street, Baltimore, MD 21218; (301) 235-8600; Kate Hopkins, innkeeper. A historic building in a historic neighborhood. Open year-round. Twenty-six guest rooms, including suites, all with private baths; some with kitchenettes. Rates: $85–$125. Continental breakfast. Children welcome; some pets (please call); smoking permitted; major credit cards accepted. Within walking distance of Baltimore Museum of Art, one block from John Hopkins University.
DIRECTIONS: call for directions.

WASHINGTON, D.C.

Left, the latticed porch and garden. Above, some of the art nouveau collection.

LOGAN CIRCLE

Extravagantly restored

Extensively restored by two loving owners, this one-hundred-year-old Victorian mansion features original wood paneling, stained-glass niches, ornate chandeliers, and a Victorian-style lattice porch and gardens. A mecca for lovers of "Art Nouveau," its walls are covered with highly selective and artfully framed posters, prints, magazine covers, and advertising art. The hostess, a tireless collector, is constantly adding new pieces to her collection.

In addition to the house's own beautiful appointments, the owners have incorporated some Victorian gems rescued by architectural salvagers: gilded mirrors, intricately carved mantels, and glistening English tiles. Floral patterns combine with silks, violet walls, wainscoting, draperies, oriental rugs, Eastlake furniture, and vintage floors, creating a romantic ambiance. One of two parlors houses a working player piano with silk-fringed turquoise shawl.

Each of the five guest rooms is singular and charming. An additional ground floor apartment offers complete privacy and comfort. Guest room furnishings include antique quilts, wicker, greenery, shutters, wash bowls, a Jacobean desk, and a four poster bed.

Overlooking a fountain and rose arbor, the latticed porch seduces with a promise to banish worldly cares. Here one can effortlessly return to the romance and elegance of by-gone days.

LOGAN CIRCLE. Century-old Victorian mansion with gardens, terrace, and Victorian-style lattice porch. Open year-round. Four guest rooms, one with private bath; apartment with private bath. Rates: $45-$55 single, $55-$65 double, apartment $60 single, $70 double. Continental breakfast included. Children welcome; no pets; smoking permitted; MasterCard/Visa/American Express. Logan Circle is an area in transition; guests are advised to drive rather than walk at night. *Represented by Bed 'n Breakfast Ltd. of Washington, D.C.*

Left and above, a collector's blend of Oriental art and French furniture.

DUPONT CIRCLE

A home becomes a work of art

Only one-half block from the famous Phillips Collection and one block from the DuPont Circle Metro, this spacious townhouse, furnished with an eclectic mix of fine Chinese, Middle Eastern, and European *objects d'art*, is a fascinating study in itself. Having pursued the arts all of her life, the hostess specializes in creating bejeweled icons, a selection of which adorns the staircase wall leading to the second-floor guest rooms. Each bedroom has a warm personality and is equipped with refrigerator, television, and even a buzzer for ordering breakfast. This meal is another work of art. Two house specialties, a carmelized French toast and savory chicken-liver omelet, are worth a special trip. The neighborhood's tree-lined streets are filled with pubs, cafés, bookstores, and specialty shops.

DUPONT CIRCLE . Century-old townhouse with lovely décor. Open year-round. Two guest rooms on second floor and, upon occasion, 2-room suite available in basement. Rates: $45 single, $60 double. Full breakfast. Children in basement suite only; no pets. In DuPont Circle area, near park and within walking distance of Georgetown. *Represented by Sweet Dreams & Toast, Inc., Washington, D.C.*

FRIENDSHIP HEIGHTS

Comfort and privacy

Custom designed by its owners five years ago, this Federal-style brick house has an enclosed garden and heated pool. The pool, uncommon to most houses in the district, offers a happy solution to Washington's steamy summers.

Plush carpeting, dark woods, Chinoiserie, and a potted palm enrich the dining room, where a generous buffet breakfast is laid.

The guest room on the lower level, with a working fireplace, is next to a game room outfitted with a pool table, pinball machine, working Victorola, and exercise bike. The guest room on the upper level is next to a sitting room with an interesting assortment of books, TV, and potted palm.

FRIENDSHIP HEIGHTS. Federal-style brick house. Open year-round. Two guest rooms, each with private bath. Rates: $50 single, $60 double. Expanded continental breakfast included. Children accepted; no pets; smoking downstairs only; MasterCard/Visa/American Express. Metro is ten-minute walk. *Represented by Bed 'n Breakfast Ltd. of Washington, D.C.*

Looking onto the sun porch.

DUPONT CIRCLE AREA

Easy friendliness

The host, affectionately called "The Muffin King" by his wife, looks forward to weekends at home when he can prepare full breakfasts that include such temptations as Swiss eggs, French toast, sautéed pears, and pina colada, pineapple coconut, or creamed corn muffins.

After falling in love with old houses—The Mainstay in particular—the hosts purchased this fabulous big house. Still intact are its red Georgian pine floors, many fireplaces with original mantels, pocket doors, and window shutters.

The hosts, husband and wife, who are both lawyers, miraculously restored and decorated the entirety in a scant six weeks. Eastlake furniture and Oriental carpets, Bradbury and Bradbury Victorian wallpaper, velvet cornices and draperies, silver service: all were purchased and installed by the two young owners to create an atmosphere that is friendly and sociable.

DUPONT CIRCLE AREA. 1903 Romanesque Revival house. Open year-round. Five guest rooms, all with private baths. Rates: $50-$70 single, $60-$80 double. Continental breakfast weekdays, full breakfast on weekends. No children; no pets; no smoking; MasterCard/Visa/American Express. *Represented by Bed 'n Breakfast Ltd. of Washington, D.C.*

CAPITOL HILL

Bed and breakfast service *par excellence*

Close to the Smithsonian Institution, the Capitol Building, and the famous monuments and government buildings, this townhouse is the home of a professional management consultant, who operates a catering service and who lived in Alaska for thirteen years. She loves to entertain, and her guests are the lucky beneficiaries of that talent. Besides making people comfortable, she also proficiently guides visitors through the ins-and-outs of Washington.

CAPITOL HILL . 1891 townhouse with stunning architectural details, private backyard and patio. Open year-round. Rates $43 single, $55 double. From one to three guest rooms, depending on family then at home; shared bath. Continental breakfast. Inquire about pets. In Capitol Hill neighborhood, close to all government centers, monuments, and the Smithsonian Institution. *Represented by Sweet Dreams & Toast, Inc., Washington, DC.*

Formal dining room set for breakfast, above. Flanking the fireplace, right, is part of the Lladro figurine collection.

Staircase leading to the guest rooms.

CHEVY CHASE

Antiques-filled modern townhouse

The owners of this splendid contemporary townhouse make guests feel as if they are in their own home. During the week, visitors may prepare their own breakfast, if they wish, and afterwards sun themselves on the private patio or bicycle through the adjoining park. The displays of Spanish art and a magnificent collection of Lladro figurines are complemented by fine antique furnishings.

CHEVY CHASE. Spacious, English-style townhouse in townhouse community. Open year-round. Rates: $40 single, $55 double. Full breakfast, prepared by guests during the week. Well-behaved pets only. In Chevy Chase, Maryland; all of Washington is accessible by car. *Represented by Sweet Dreams & Toast, Inc., Washington, DC.*

BED & BREAKFAST
IN THE COUNTRY

MAINE

CLEFTSTONE MANOR

Preserves the mood of Victorian gentility

James Blair built his summer home, a modest thirty-three room cottage, high on a rocky ledge overlooking the beautiful isle of Bar Harbor. His winter home in Washington, D.C., later used as an alternate presidential residence known as Blair House, sat across from the White House. Today both homes welcome travelers, Blair House serving as a home to dignitaries visiting the United States. Cleftstone Manor, under the thoughtful ownership of Phyllis and Donald Jackson, is a supremely lovely bed and breakfast inn.

The entire house is furnished with fine antiques, including such unusual pieces as Joseph Pulitzer's awesome writing table. This grand table amply fills the formal dining room and is put to use each day when it is laden with scones and shortbread at tea time and with cheeses and wine in the evening. Bre[...] sunporch, a l[...] white wicker [...] and masses [...]

The bedr[...] with a co[...] favorite for [...] and Juliet Room [...] brass canopied bed, draped in [...] comfortable love seat faces a working fireplace and the beautifully detailed coffered ceiling deepens the prevailing sense of privacy and luxury. The Glastonbury Room, with high-back Victorian bedstead, red velvet chair, hand-crocheted bedspread, and many decorative grace notes is serene.

CLEFTSTONE MANOR, Eden St., Bar Harbor, ME 04609; (207) 288-4951; Phyllis and Donald Jackson and family, hosts. Open May 15 to Oct. 15. Eighteen double rooms, four with fireplaces, one with balcony; two family suites; mostly private baths. Rates: $35 to $60 double, shared baths, $70 to $100, private baths; rates include breakfast with emphasis on home baking. Four-o'clock tea daily; evening wine and cheese. Numerous restaurants nearby. Children welcome; no pets; Visa/MasterCard/American Express. Owner's son operates hot-air ballooning business at inn.

DIRECTIONS: from points south, take Rte. 1 north to Ellsworth, then follow Rte. 3 into Bar Harbor. Inn is 500 feet past Bluenose Ferry terminal.

Left, the Romeo and Juliet honeymoon suite. Above, Joseph Pulitzer's writing table in the formal dining room.

An extraordinary stone mansion

Norumbega is an extraordinary stone mansion whose elusive exterior seems to change when viewed at different angles. Designed by A.B. Jennings of New York City, the Queen Anne style manse is quite unique. From one angle the house shows a wall of roughly faced cobblestones, punctuated by arched windows and a rounded, stepped roof. From another, it resembles a more common seaside cottage with a wide porch and bay windows. Looking at the entrance, the *porte cochere*, and turret, the structure appears to be predominantly wood and brick. Close inspection

reveals at least three different shingle patterns on the turret, the name "Norumbega" and "1886" tiled and set in the right bay, and fossils embedded in the stone to the left of the entrance.

Inside, the wood draws first notice. Triangular-sawn oak with a marked sheen forms the entryway and three stairs to a landing with fireplace and elaborately carved corner seating. Spiral spindles below the banister add a suitably delicate touch.

The double parlors and curved study boast their share of beautiful wood. Carved grotesques, as compelling as Notre Dame's gargoyles, flank the fireplace; a central wood carpet establishes the floor theme.

Norumbega's eccentricities are attributable to its creator, Joseph Stearns, an inventor who made his fortune by patenting the "duplex system," a system by which two messages could be relayed by telegraph simultaneously.

Stearns was a man ahead of his time. He commissioned an astronomical observatory (now gone), a room to hold one hundred tons of coal, and a darkroom. By the time Mark Boland bought Norumbega, carpenter ants had eaten a floor in the basement, upstairs wall lathes, and some beams. The house, now restored to its full elegance, is a stunning, hospitable, and gracious home complete with mountain and water views.

NORUMBEGA, 61 High St., Camden, ME 04843; (207) 236-4646; V. Mark Boland, host. Open all year except Christmas. Seven guest rooms, all with private baths, three with working fireplaces. Rates: $110 to $140; additional person, $45; includes generous, full breakfast. Children over 12 welcome; no pets; no smoking; no credit cards. Hiking, skiing, tennis, golf, ocean beach and freshwater lake, windjammer cruises, Lighthouse Museum in Rockland. Good restaurants.

DIRECTIONS: follow Rte. 1 north through Camden. The inn is on the right about one mile from town.

Left, the original reception hall. Above, a light and airy guest room.

Beamed ceilings and a 200-year-old cherry mantel.

KENNISTON HILL INN

Once a country club

The seventeen-mile-long Boothbay Peninsula extends into the ocean like a three-pronged fork, defined on either side by the Sheepscot and Damariscotta rivers. Newagen, one of the more established enclaves of seaside Maine, forms the point of the west tine. Ocean Point, with its scenic views, perches at the eastern tip in territory once frequented by Captain Kidd. The lively tourist haven of Boothbay Harbor lies in the middle.

A mile from the harbor, Kenniston Hill stands back from the street at the end of a narrow allé of maple and oak trees. This center-chimney colonial dates from 1786 when the prosperous Kenniston family moved in and established residence for almost a hundred years. The next notable owner acquired the house in 1922 and developed it as a clubhouse for the new Boothbay Country Club which still owns grounds adjacent to Kenniston Hill. After a brief time as an apartment house, the gracious building became an inn in 1956.

History helps make the inn a special place. Three separate entrances from its days as an apartment house add a welcome bit of privacy. Still, guests often choose to gather in front of the living room fireplace. The three-hundred-year-old cherry mantelpiece forms a nesting place for wooden ducks and assorted baskets. A collection of handmade and acquired stained glass light-catchers decorate the paned window wall.

Paul and Ellen Morisette retired to Kenniston Hill, giving up their Country Kitchen restaurant in Brattleboro, Vermont. "It's never humid here like Vermont. We don't need air conditioning. The windows are always open for breezes," Ellen says happily, "and now we have time to talk to people." They also have time to prepare an outstanding breakfast of such fare as delicately sauced eggs Benedict, fresh asparagus, and fluffy light popovers. Artfully presented fresh fruit pleases the eye as well as the palate.

The breakfast room, like most of the house, is furnished simply in deference to the colonial tradition. Pale yellow pineapple paper picks up the soft specks of gold and brown in the braided rug and the tawny hues of the pine sideboard. What makes Kenniston Hill most appealing, though, are the four guest rooms with working fireplace. A modest idyll, Kenniston Hill is perfect for all-season beachcombers and high-season sailors.

KENNISTON HILL INN, Rte. 27, Boothbay, ME 04537; (207) 633-2159; Paul and Ellen Morisette, hosts. Open April through December. White clapboard colonial built in 1786, on 4½ acres. Eight guest rooms, four with working fireplaces, five with private baths. Rates: $40 to $70, single; $45 to $75, double; $10 for additional person. Full breakfast served. Children over ten preferred; no pets; MasterCard/Visa. Bicycles available at no charge; 9-hole golf nearby. Varied dining at the harbor.

DIRECTIONS: from Rte. 1 turn onto Rte. 27 south to Boothbay. The inn is on a knoll on the left.

ENGLISH MEADOWS INN

Like a visit to Grandma's

Gene Kelly bought Gussie English's country boarding house with a mind to renting out a room or two for a little extra income. Never in his wildest dreams did he imagine the devoted following that English Meadows Inn would inspire.

The inn sits on rolling and wooded acreage that still feels like country, though today the property dovetails with Kennebunkport's commercial center. Century-old lilacs, which perform gorgeously and fragrantly each spring, provide a curtain of privacy for the inn. Rooms in the main house are filled with antiques, rag and hooked rugs, and beautiful old patchwork quilts. Additional guest quarters in the adjoining rustic barn combine knotty pine, an open fireplace, wicker furniture, and views of field and garden to create a comfortable camplike atmosphere.

Behind the inn, and nestled in a pine grove, is an "enchanted" cottage. With its own full kitchen, dining room, and bedroom, it offers perfect solitude.

Breakfast prepared by Claudia is ample and delicious. One guest was so enamored of her sour dough French toast and maple syrup that he changed clothes, donned dark glasses, and seated himself for a second round. The poor fellow was found out, but the compliment was appreciated nonetheless.

Buttons, the inn's shaggy top dog, completes the scene and occasionally upstages Gene and Claudia, whose mutual senses of humor defy succinct description. Suffice it to say, Archie Bunker could take lessons from Gene.

ENGLISH MEADOWS INN, R.F.D. #1, Rte. 35, Kennebunkport, ME 04046; (207) 967-5766; Gene Kelly and Claudia Kelly Butler, hosts. A stay at this *circa* 1860 Victorian farmhouse is like a visit to Grandma's. Open April 1 through October, and weekends all year. Fourteen guest rooms with semi-private baths; two apartments. Rates: $40 to $42 single, $65 to $68 double, varying seasonally; apartments $400 to $500 and cottage $600 per week, monthly rates available; rates include "famous" breakfast. Excellent dining nearby, especially seafood. No children under twelve; no pets; no credit cards. Maine coast is vacationer's dream for recreation, scenery, historic sites.

DIRECTIONS: take Maine Turnpike to exit 3 (Kennebunk). Turn left on Rte. 35 south. Inn is five miles ahead on right.

Guests like to make themselves at home in the living room.

Breakfast room in the main house.

OLD FORT INN

Kennebunkport charm

The Old Fort Inn is a charming carriage house-lodge combination that invites travelers for long-term stays. The fourteen color-coordinated American and English country-style rooms come with color television, extra bed, efficiency kitchens stocked with ironstone plates, wine glasses, pans, tea kettle, toaster, napkins and placemats—even laundry facilities.

It's one-and-a-half miles from the inn to town, an easy bike ride past lovely frame cottages and old sea captains' houses. Kennebunkport retains much of its late nineteenth-century atmosphere when ship building gave way to the tourist industry. Wealthy summer visitors built wisely and well, keeping the village quaint and relatively small. The inn's location, just a few blocks from the rocky shore, is also adjacent to Cape Arundel, where some of the most handsome turn-of-the-century cottages still stand.

Kennebunkport offers a rich variety of activities: trolley rides, scenic cruises, sailing lessons, yacht charters, and whale watching are but a few. The sports menu complements what the Old Fort Inn has to offer on its grounds. A swimming pool, shuffleboard area, and tennis court bridge the gap between the guest rooms and the main lodge where breakfast is served.

Sheila and David Aldrich and their daughter oversee the homemade muffins and fresh-baked breads for the continental breakfast. Friendships often begin at the morning meal and extend into the evening hours around the pool.

The Old Fort Inn presents the best of what casual adult resorts can provide: a relaxed atmosphere amid pleasant surroundings.

OLD FORT INN, Old Fort Ave., Kennebunkport, ME 04046; (207) 967-5353; Sheila and David Aldrich, hosts. Open April 26 to mid-December. Fourteen guest rooms, all with private baths and efficiency kitchens. Rates: $70 to $92; suites, $115; additional person, $15. Rates include continental breakfast and one hour of tennis daily. Children over 6 welcome; no pets; no smoking in the bedrooms; American Express/MasterCard/Visa. Area attractions; good restaurants. Antiques shop in main lodge.

DIRECTIONS: take exit 3 (Kennebunkport) from the Maine Turnpike, then take a left on Rte. 35 and follow signs through Kennebunk to Kennebunkport. Take a left at the traffic light at the Sunoco station. Go over the drawbridge and take the first right onto Ocean Ave. Take Ocean Ave. to the Colony Hotel, turn left in front of the Colony, go to the Y in the road and take the right branch ¼ mile. The inn is on the left.

Each guest room has a kitchenette.

A spacious third-floor guest room

CAPTAIN JEFFERDS INN

A New England sea captain's house

The Kennebunkport historic district is peppered with gracious "cottages" built in the early 1800s by seafaring captains who traveled the globe in pursuit of treasure.

Warren Fitzsimmons and Don Kelly were partners in a successful antiques business when they bought one of these—Captain Jefferds' home—and brought the place to vibrant life. If, upon entering, you have a sense of déjà vu, don't doubt your feelings. The work of these two gifted innkeepers has been featured on the covers of several prestigious home decorating magazines. Two cobalt blue vases displaying a bounty of brilliant silk flowers flank the formal entryway. To the left is the breakfast room where guests gather each morning to be served by Don, dressed in butler's whites. Warren mans the kitchen, serving up custardy French toast, delicate pancakes, and perfectly turned eggs.

Each bedroom is special. Several are decorated in Laura Ashley's simple prints; others are dressed in muted tones that dramatize an elegant chaise, bird's-eye maple chest, or Chinese screen.

The collection of antiques in this inn is endlessly fascinating. Warren and Don buy only the truest examples of a representative period—there are no reproductions in the entire inn—and the place practically vibrates from the beauty produced by their combined collections. Though Warren and Don were personally attracted to American antiques, from tramp and shell art to twig furniture and Indian baskets, the inn's formal lines required sterling silver and crystal as well. It all works.

THE CAPTAIN JEFFERDS INN, Pearl St., Box 691, Kennebunkport, ME 04046; (207) 967-2311; Don Kelly and Warren Fitzsimmons, hosts. 1804 Federal style sea captain's house. Open all year except Christmas Eve and Day, with weekday closings during winter months. Twelve guest rooms in main house, mostly private baths; three efficiency apartments in carriage house. Rates $45 single, $65 to $85 double; apartments $500 to $750 per week, in season; guests in main house are treated to full breakfast, with seasonal specialties. No children under twelve; pets welcome, with advance notice; smoking restricted; no credit cards.

DIRECTIONS: take Maine Turnpike to exit 3 to Rte. 35. Follow signs through Kennebunk to Kennebunkport. Turn left at traffic light and cross drawbridge. Turn right at monument onto Ocean Ave. Proceed ³⁄₁₀ mile to Arundel Wharf and turn left onto Pearl St.

WOODEN GOOSE INN

A stunning restoration

Right off Route 1, sometimes called the "antique row of New England," the Wooden Goose Inn corners off its own country garden in full view of the Cape Neddick River. Guests gazing out from the glassed-in breakfast room overlook the perennial blooms and a specially commissioned Chippendale garden bench. The bench is just one of interior designer Jerry Rippetoe's unique additions to this intimate country house. Partner Tony Sienicki, the other half of this able team, attends to most of the carpentry and finishing.

The precision restoration began June 15, 1983, the day they bought the house. By July 2, after working twenty-two-hour days, Jerry and Tony welcomed their first overnight visitors. The quick revitalization succeeded only because of professional foresight and months of planning and preparation. "The day we looked at it we took measurements," remarked Tony.

The result is stunning. A true overabundance of Victorian paraphernalia blends with revitalized Orientalia. The focus in the reception room rests

on the hand-carved, hand-painted cormondel screen, a black lacquer on teak *chef-d'oeuvre* that hints at other treasures inside. Guests are rarely disappointed with the many beautiful touches.

Excess and elegance are synonymous here. Twenty-eight yards of chintz drape down from one canopy. The clawfoot tub of bedroom number 4 stands in regal spaciousness next to a bentwood rocker, a combination that inspires guests to bring their own bubble bath and champagne.

Morning starts with elaborate breakfasts served on Lenox china with silver and linen asides. Plans to replace Sheelan crystal with Waterford illustrate the dynamics of the Wooden Goose. Every January the doors close for redecoration. Balloon shades change to miniblinds; greens give way to blues. The transformation keeps the inn vital—and keeps guests returning year after year.

THE WOODEN GOOSE INN, Rte. 1, Cape Neddick, ME 03902; (207) 363-5673; Tony Sienicki and Jerry Rippetoe, hosts. Some French spoken. Open February through December. Six guest rooms, all with private baths. Rates: $ including an elegant, hearty breakfast w Dining nearby. Children over 12 welc cards. The ocean is one mile from the bicycling in Ogunquit.

DIRECTIONS: take I-95 to the York ex exit before toll"). Turn north on Rte. 1 is on the right, five houses after the junc

Left, the whole house is full of exquisite bric-a-brac.

NEW HAMPSHIRE

THE INN AT CHRISTIAN SHORE

Make yourself at home

The Inn at Christian Shore offers visitors to historic Portsmouth an opportunity to relax in one of the city's historic homes and partake of one of the grandest breakfasts anywhere.

After applying considerable energy and talent to the restoration of this sea captain's home, Louis Sochia, Thomas Towey, and Charles Litchfield opened their cozy and comfortable house to the public. The dining room is particularly charming with exposed beams, dark blue wainscoting, open fireplace, harvest table and Hitchcock chairs, and attractively displayed antique prints and primitive paintings.

Breakfast begins with juice or fresh fruit in season and a warm fruit loaf, possibly Tom's special banana-blueberry bread. Next, guests are served an egg dish and steak, pork tenderloin, or ham fried with pineapple. This substantial "main course" is always accompanied by home-fried potatoes and a vegetable in season—broccoli, cauliflower, or possibly steamed squash—a slice of tomato on a bed of lettuce, toast, and a hot beverage.

Though after such bounteous fare, food is not foremost in one's mind, Portsmouth offers an amazing array of wonderful restaurants. A short distance from the inn is the renowned Blue Strawberry, which is noted for skillfully prepared dishes created by a chef of rare talent and ingenuity.

THE INN AT CHRISTIAN SHORE, 335 Maplewood Ave., Portsmouth, NH 03801; (603) 431-6770; Charles Litchfield, Thomas Towey, and Louis Sochia, hosts. Sea captain's house, Federal style *circa* 1800. Open all year. Six guest rooms, including one single; private and shared baths. Rates: $30 single all year, $55 to $60 double, including exceptionally extravagant breakfast. Wine served in afternoon. Good restaurants within walking distance. Children over 12 welcome; no pets; no credit cards; personal checks accepted.

DIRECTIONS: from Boston, take I-95 to exit 5 and proceed to Portsmouth Rotary Circle. Drive halfway around to Rte. 1, proceeding north to Maplewood Ave. exit (last exit before bridge) and turn right. Inn is sixth house on left. Parking behind house.

Host Louis Sochia in the living room.

MOOSE MOUNTAIN LODGE

Casual, with lots of fireplaces

Moose Moutain Lodge virtually spills over the western slope of Moose Mountain. Porch-sitters recline in full view of unspoiled countryside, where Vermont's Green Mountains rise out of the clear, smooth-running waters of the Connecticut River.

Just a dozen or so miles northeast of Hanover, home of Dartmouth College, the lodge is a back-country hideaway on forty acres, situated on a dirt cul de sac that ends at the top of a ridge. Between the lodge and the mountaintop the road is veined with numerous trails, far away from the whoosh of passing traffic and noisy crowds. Winter skiers and summer hikers can disappear into the woods and feel secluded.

Inside, Kay and Peter Shumway cater to nature-lovers who gather around one of three common-room fireplaces. The stone fireplace in the living room warms-up conversation as much as it does noses and toes.

"You can put your feet up here. We love tracked-in snow!" says Kay, who emphasizes that her guests relax without thinking about ruining the floors or spilling a drink. Somehow, the Shumways still manage to keep the lodge fresh, clean, and comfortable.

After dinner many folks head down to the bar room (BYOB) to play ping-pong, darts, or a board game by yet another native stone fireplace, this one mottled with garnet-studded rose quartz. A working player piano livens up the evening with classic old favorites. Once the music's over, guests retire to appropriately rustic bedrooms made especially homey with handmade spruce log or other wooden beds and muted Marimekko linens.

MOOSE MOUNTAIN LODGE, Etna, NH 03750; (603) 643-3529; Kay and Peter Shumway, innkeepers. Open January to April and June to November. Twelve cozy rooms share five modern bathrooms plus two tiled bathrooms in common rooms. Hearty breakfast. Rates: $30 per person plus 10% service charge. Dinners are offered year-round to guests only for an additional $15 per person. Children over 5 are welcome; no pets; limited smoking. 50 km of cross-country ski trails; downhill skiing within 10 miles; hiking trails. Dartmouth College offers cultural events year-round.

DIRECTIONS: from exit 18 on Rte. 89, go north on Rte. 120 toward Hanover, ½ mile. Higbea Motel and Lander's Restaurant are on the left. Turn right here onto Etna Rd. into Etna Village. Go ½ mile past the Etna Store (phone from here if it's your first time) and turn right onto Rudsboro Rd. (just before the church. Go up Rudsboro Rd. 2 miles, then turn left on Dana Rd. Continue on Dana Rd. for ½ mile. Turn right. Drive up the mountain one mile to the Lodge.

WHITE GOOSE INN

Cozy American with European panache

Orford is seated by the banks of the upper Connecticut River just across a bridge from Fairlee, Vermont. Originally a "fort town" built by the British, it soon hummed with activity from logging and agriculture. Seven "ridge houses" dating from between 1773 and 1839 form a stately white row by the green in the town's center.

The White Goose Inn is also celebrated for its elm tree growing through the circular colonial revival porch. Manfred and Karin Wolf adopted this brick and woodframe home and transformed it into a cozy American country classic with European panache.

Karin, a craftsperson whose work is evident throughout the inn, did all the delicate stenciling, made the pierced parchment lampshades, and cunningly assembled traveler's sewing kits for each impeccably designed, spotless guest room.

White geese are the house motif. A porcelain goose with a pink satin ribbon around its neck sits in the window; a cloth goose pokes its head out of a basket on the hutch; and an early American metal cut-out depicts a young girl followed by two geese. And there's a white wooden goose on the marble-topped treadle sewing machine base in the hall to greet guests when they arrive.

Breakfasts are very special here, reflecting the hosts' European heritage. Hearty home-baked goods look even more tempting on the Wolf's fine china.

The tasteful choices in furnishing and accessories are consistent throughout the White Goose. The parlor exudes the glow from an unusual porcelain chandelier. The dining room benefits from a beautifully crafted modern wood table and tall Shaker-style chairs.

This wonderful hideaway engages its guests, tempting them again and again to relax and sit back in an attractive setting where the details in every room please the eye.

THE WHITE GOOSE INN, Rte. 10, P.O. Box 17, Orford, NH 03777; (603) 353-4812; Manfred and Karin Wolf. German spoken. Open all year. Eight guest rooms with private and shared baths. Rates; $55 to $75, including a country breakfast. Children under 8 discouraged; no pets; smoking only in the bedrooms. MasterCard/Visa. Hiking, biking trails, golf, skiing, sleigh rides; Saint-Gaudens National Historic Site. Dartmouth College, 15 miles.

DIRECTIONS: from I-91, take exit 15 (Fairlee, VT); cross the bridge to New Hampshire and take Rte. 10 south one mile. The inn is on the left. From I-93, take exit for I-89 and continue to Rte. 10 north. The inn is approximately 15 miles north of Hanover on the right.

Collecting maple syrup from the inn's own trees.

CRAB APPLE INN

With an English country garden

Crab Apple Inn is charming—from its well-preserved doorway fan to its babbling brook. White trim and black shutters complement the 1835 brick Federal building and the white picket fence that encloses the tidy house and its brilliantly colored English country garden.

Two cheery third-floor rooms boast the best view, overlooking most of the inn's two-and-a-half acres and Crosby Mountain. Yet every guest gets something special: an arched canopy bed, a hand-carved sleigh bed, a brass bed. Intimate and cozy, the household harbors a warmth that emanates primarily from its two owners, Carolyn and Bill Crenson, who had been planning to open a bed and breakfast for years.

An award-winning sign.

When they moved in, they took over management of the inn. "It was twenty below. Pipes were freezing, snow, wind. And we had guests two days later—a full house," recounts Carolyn.

This is indeed snow country, the gateway to the White Mountains. Polar Caves is one mile down the road, and Waterville Valley and Tenney Mountain, minutes away.

Warm weather enthusiasts can wade in nearby Newfound Lake or relax on the brick patio, sipping iced tea by the French doors, with candy and fresh fruit available. Breakfasts, whether indoors or *al fresco*, feature refreshingly simple, home-cooked country fare.

Carolyn and Bill attend to the small details that make life more enjoyable when on the road—leaving terry cloth robes for those guests in rooms with shared baths and offering wine or tea and snacks in the afternoon.

CRAB APPLE INN, Rte. 25, RFD 2, Box 200B, West Plymouth, NH 03264; (603) 536-4476; Carolyn and Bill Crenson, innkeepers. Open all year. Five guest rooms; suite and one bedroom have private bath; two rooms share one bath. Rates: $50 to $65, including a country breakfast. Children over 8 welcome; no pets. MasterCard/Visa. All-season recreation in area; antiquing. Good restaurants nearby.

DIRECTIONS: from I-93, take exit 26 and head west on Rte. 25. The inn is 4 miles from the interstate on the left.

". . . and the snow lay round about, deep and crisp and even."

HAVERHILL INN

1810 Federal house near village green

In its heyday, Haverhill was a county seat, and prosperity left its mark in the form of grand mansions, many sitting high on the rise overlooking the lovely Connecticut River and Vermont's rolling hills. When the railroad bypassed Haverhill, the town stood still. Today you can't find a grocery, drug store, or even a general store. "Modernization" has never touched this island of beauty, and Haverhill is richer for its loss.

The Haverhill Inn is one of those elegantly proportioned mansions that overlooks the river. It emanates a calm and tranquility that speaks well of its keepers, Katharine DeBoer and Stephen Campbell. But this peaceful atmosphere can also be traced to older inhabitants. Three volumes of data and letters have been compiled on the history of Haverhill and the house. Tracing its lineage,

readers discover that each owner bestowed genuine love on this home. This fortunate history has left its mark.

Today the inn comprises four guest rooms. Each is spacious and each has a working fireplace. The living room, which contains Katharine's baby grand piano, is a comfortable gathering spot, where guests can enjoy a glass of sherry, cup of tea, or a good read. Both Katharine and Stephen pursue careers outside innkeeping. She is a soloist soprano, who gives concerts and teaches. Stephen has a thriving career as a computer programming consultant. Since most of their work is done out of their home, the inn is always well tended.

In summer Katharine plants a large garden from which guests enjoy a bounty of fresh produce. Stephen is a dedicated and gifted cook who makes breakfast a very special event, especially on Sunday.

HAVERHILL INN, Dartmouth College Hwy., Rte. 10, Haverhill, NH 03765; (603) 989-5961; Stephen Campbell and Katharine DeBoer, hosts. French spoken. 1810 Federal style house on quiet street near village green. Open all year. Four guest rooms, all private baths. Rates: $50 single, $65 double, with $10 per additional occupant, including full breakfast. Afternoon tea and coffee. Restaurants nearby. Older children welcome; pets discouraged; smoking restricted; no credit cards.

DIRECTIONS: from Hanover, take Rte. 10 North 27 miles. From NYC (6 hrs.), take I-91 North to exit 15 (Fairlee, Vt.), cross river to Orford, N.H., and proceed north on Rte. 10. From Boston, I-93 to Plymouth, Rte. 25 west to Haverhill.

BEAL HOUSE INN

Candlelit breakfasts

The Beal House Inn feels more like a sociable country inn than does the average bed and breakfast. Doug and Brenda Clickenger operate a warm and cheerful hostelry, one that welcomes guests into comfortable common rooms filled with books and magazines, and bedrooms decorated generously with antiques. The intrinsic charm of The Beal House, besides being a reflection of thoughtful ownership, is due to the fact that the entire inn is an antiques shop. With the exception of a collection of rugs original to the inn and a few select items, everything you look at, sleep atop, sit in, or admire is for sale. What finer way to shop for a bed or chair than to live with it for a time. An antiques shop/inn makes for an ever-changing decor, since a room that loses its elaborate Victorian canopied bed might in turn gain a weighty sleigh bed or a pair of simple pencil post twins.

The Beal House Inn is located at the foot of Littleton's Main Street, where it serves as a graceful transition between shops and residences. An extension of downtown, the inn feels Littleton's pulse, and residents love to visit, especially in the morning when Doug's breakfast is served to guests and public alike. Because it is the only meal they serve, the Clickengers go out of their way to make it a memorable occasion. The dining room is candlelit, and Brenda dresses in old-fashioned garb reminiscent of the mid-1800s, when the inn was a farmhouse on the edge of town. Doug has gained a reputation for both his extra-creamy scrambled eggs, served piping hot in a glass hen, and his towering popovers. Each morning the dining room is the center of activity. This quiet bustle lends to the Beal House the kind of cozy atmosphere that is the hallmark of all successful country inns.

THE BEAL HOUSE INN, Main St., Littleton, NH 03561; (603) 444-2661; Clickenger family, hosts. Frame Federal-style house has been inn-*cum*-antiques-shop for over 50 years. Open all year. Fifteen guest rooms, ten with private baths. Rates $35 to $70, according to season and amenities. Additional charge for full country breakfast served tavern-style. Evening tea and snacks. Current menus and reservation service for local dining. Children welcome; pet boarding nearby; smoking restricted; major credit cards.

DIRECTIONS: from I-93, take exit 41 into Littleton. Turn left onto Main St. to inn, at junction of Rtes. 18 and 302.

Left, the staircase leading to the guest rooms is bedecked with whimsical bookends and doorstops.

VERMONT

PARMENTER HOUSE

Wonderful hosts in the back country

Cynthia and Lester Firschein, both anthropologists, have turned the Parmenter House into a backcountry hiker's dream. Hikers themselves, they have made it their business to acquaint themselves with the dirt roads and paths around Belmont, which include trail heads for the Long and Appalachian trails. Cynthia knows of at least ten day-hike segments within half an hour of their house. Opting for a more speedy tour, guests can rent trail bikes at the inn for $25 a day. The rate covers a generous box lunch and being picked up at the end of the day. Cynthia and Lester have made copies of their favorite routes: to an herb farm; along Towner Road (the most photographed road in Vermont); and to a music camp that offers classical concerts.

Guests often take breakfast on the deck out back. Afternoon tea is served in the Eastlake-inspired living room amid paintings and screens by Alfred Rasmussen, Cynthia's grandfather. Her mother carved the walnut dining room set, and her uncles painted the trunk in which her grandmother brought her belongings from Denmark.

The appeal of the Parmenter House, however, lies with its laid-back hosts, who will spontaneously gather a group for a caravan ride and picnic or take guests to visit the Weston Priority, a serenely picturesque Benedictine monastery.

THE PARMENTER HOUSE, P.O. Box 106, Belmont, VT 05730; (802) 259-2009; Cynthia and Lester Firschein, hosts. Spanish and French spoken. Open all year. Five guest rooms, one with private bath. Rates; $40 to $75; additional person, $15. Includes continental breakfast. MasterCard/Visa for deposits only. Theater, many outdoor activities, Ludlow restaurants nearby.

DIRECTIONS: from I-91, take exit 6 and then Rte. 103 through Chester and Ludlow. After Ludlow center and Okemo Access Road (which will be on left), stay on Rte. 103 until you come to a blinking light. Turn left at this light. After two miles you will come to the center of Belmont, marked by a four-cornered intersection. Turn left; the Parmenter House is the second house on your left, directly opposite the white church.

Left, tea in the parlor, amid the Bradbury and Bradbury wallpaper. Above, innkeeper Cynthia Firschein at breakfast.

SHOREHAM INN AND COUNTRY STORE

A tiny town on Lake Champlain

Surrounded by apple orchards and dairy farms, and bordered on one side by Lake Champlain's sinuous tail, the Shoreham Inn and its adjoining Country Store form the heart of tiny Shoreham, Vermont. The inn's atmosphere, reflecting its beautiful setting and kind proprietors, is warm, gentle, and welcoming.

Built in 1799 as a public house, it allows today's inngoers to walk the same wooden floorboards that its first visitors trod. These wide planks are partially hidden by lustrous old area rugs and an irregular collection of antiques—none matches, but all work together—that please the eye and comfort the spirit.

Cleo and Fred Alter love original art, a taste fully developed during the days they worked together in printing and graphic design, and they exercise this love by showing the work of gifted local artists. Not a gallery per se, the inn doesn't sell work but the Alters do take pleasure in sharing beautiful things with others.

Breakfast is low-keyed. On each table guests find a canning jar filled with granola, pitchers of milk and juice, local honey and preserves, muffins or scones, and cheese. Since this is apple country, Cleo always serves the fruit in one form or another. Glass cookie jars in the center of each large dining table are always stocked with homebaked sweets for snackers.

The Country Store, just next to the inn, supplies everything from magazines and groceries to hardware and wine. The Alters operate a small delicatessen in back, where you can order a pizza or sandwiches and salads. Picnic tables on the village green beckon on a summer day.

SHOREHAM INN AND COUNTRY STORE, Shoreham, VT 05770; (802) 897-5081; Cleo and Fred Alter, hosts. Built as an inn in 1799, the Shoreham served as a way station for floating railroad bridge and ferry across Lake Champlain. Open all year. Eleven guest rooms, some accommodating four people, shared baths. Rates $35 single, $50 double, including country breakfast. Numerous restaurants in area. Children welcome; no pets; no credit cards. Area offers aquatic and other sports, museums, Ft. Ticonderoga, Morgan horse farm.

DIRECTIONS: inn is 12 miles southwest of Middlebury. Follow Rte. 22A from Fairhaven to Rte. 74 west. From Burlington, take 7 south to 22A at Vergennes, then take 74 west into Shoreham. Ticonderoga ferry operates to and from Shoreham.

MAPLE CREST FARM

Ancestral home and working dairy farm

Maple Crest Farm has been in the same family for five generations, ever since it opened its doors as Gleason Tavern in 1808. The resulting atmosphere is multi-layered and rich. This is not a manicured vacation resort; rather it is a working dairy farm with a hundred head of cattle.

The architectural styles in the farmhouse are interesting. Gleason built a colonial structure with Federal embellishments. Enter the Victorian age with its mandatory decorative porches and ornate hearth treatments. And finally the twentieth century brought with it inelegant linoleum and acoustical tiles. Though each age will still be represented, Donna Smith, Maple Crest's gracious hostess, is slowly but surely removing the more offensive "improvements" and uncovering original floors and beams.

Guests spend hours poring over diaries and the family bible, observing a dairy farm at work, and in the spring participating in maple-sugaring.

The dairy barns.

Acres of hiking paths become excellent cross-country ski trails when snow cooperates. All in all, Maple Crest Farm is a diamond in the rough and well worth a visit.

MAPLE CREST FARM, Box 120, Cuttingsville, VT 05738; (802) 492-3367; William and Donna Smith, hosts. Closed first two weeks of November, Thanksgiving, Christmas Eve and Day. Four guest rooms with shared bath, one two-bedroom apartment. Rates: $35 double; full breakfast included. Restaurants in nearby Rutland. Preschool children on occasion; no pets; no credit cards.

DIRECTIONS: from Manchester, take Rte. 7 north to Rte. 103 (just south of Rutland). Turn right on 103, cross railroad tracks, and drive up the hill. Watch for "Meadow Sweet Herb Farm" sign. At hilltop, bear left on Lincoln Hill Rd. and continue 2 miles; farm is in Shrewesbury on right, across from church and meeting hall.

Donna's breakfast bread.

SHIRE INN

Where guests come to relax

Chelsea sits at the junction of Routes 113 and 110, a quiet town known for its two commons, few remaining dairy farms, and Battey's General Store, the oldest—since 1794—continuously operating country store in Vermont. Nothing much seems to change these care-worn streets—neither the filming of a movie or a morning news segment or being chosen as a typical New England town for Walt Disney's Circlerama.

That's precisely why people come here. "There's really nothing to do in Chelsea but relax," says De, an unflagging host who insists on making every guest feel special. He lays the fire and provides boxloads of dry, sweet-smelling, hand-hewn wood for the guest rooms with fireplaces.

At breakfast, he dons a red tartan vest with waiter's shirt and pants, bringing out each dish of his wife Tilli's good food: a specially mixed blender drink, fresh or baked fruit, and possibly a delicate *eierkuchen*, an oven-baked puffed pancake swathed in lemon-butter sauce. "A guest who stays one week gets a different meal and a different place setting each day," notes Tilli.

Dinner is open to the public by advance reservation only, but generally the people sitting down at night to eat are overnight guests, and the feeling of being at home is preserved.

The Shire Inn specializes in congenial, relaxed informality with a backdrop of elegance. It's like an Aladdin's lamp, a little worn and tarnished, but guaranteed to grant your heart's desire.

THE SHIRE INN, P.O. Box 37, Main St., Chelsea, VT 05038; (802) 685-3031; De and Tilli Davis, innkeepers. Open all year except April and November. Federal-style brick house built in 1832. German spoken. Six guest rooms, two with private baths and fireplaces, two with washbowls and fireplaces, two with shared bath. Rates: $45, single; $50 to $65, double; additional person, $15. Higher rates in foliage season. Breakfast included; dinner is $20 extra. Children over twelve welcome; no pets; no smoking; no credit cards. Cross-country skiing, hiking, antiquing.

DIRECTIONS: from I-89 take the Sharon exit (exit 2) to Rte. 14 to S. Royalton, to Rte. 110 north to Chelsea. From I-91, take the Thetford exit (exit 14) to Rte. 113 north to Chelsea. The inn is on the village's main road, on the left.

Impeccable detailing throughout includes this tea cup collection.

THE JACKSON HOUSE AT WOODSTOCK

Elegant décor

The Jackson House at Woodstock is as friendly as it is elegant. Jack Foster greets you warmly upon arrival, offering a pair of "scuffies" as he welcomes you to the house. These comfortable slippers—and the heat lamps in the bathrooms—typify the thought that went into the formation of this bed and breakfast.

With professional flair, Jack decorated the nine guest rooms, imbuing them with a clever sense of style. This is most apparent in the Gloria Swanson Room, a yellow room with primitive maple furniture, maple floor, even a maple picture frame. A photograph of the famous actress graces the dresser. Each room is quite lovely and unique. The Wentworth has a pre-Columbian feel; Cranberry, an oriental mien. The Mary T. Lincoln is a more traditional room in walnut, while the Thornbirds appeals to ocean lovers who delight in the sea green hues and bamboo appointments.

Guests wander down to breakfast from 7:30 to 9:30, sharing conversation around a Jacobean gate-leg table that came from an English pub.

Jack prides himself on the food he serves. A standard morning entrée might be Spinach and Eggs Grisanti, a fragrant egg dish that includes spinach, garlic, and parmesan cheese, or cheese blintzes. Homemade muffins and coffeecake and the normal complement of fruit, juices, jams complete the meal.

THE JACKSON HOUSE AT WOODSTOCK, Rte. 4 West, Woodstock, VT 05091; (802) 457-2065; Jack D. Foster, host. Closed April 1 to May 15 and November 1 to December 15. Nine guest rooms, seven with private baths. Rates: $65 to $85; additional person, $20. Children over 11 welcome; no pets; no smoking. Visa/MasterCard. Robert Trent Jones golf course; tennis. French touring bikes available.

DIRECTIONS: The Jackson House is 1½ miles west of Woodstock Village on Rte. 4

Genuine antiques cast a special magic spell all their own.

THE CHARLESTON HOUSE

Southern hospitality

The Charleston House is Woodstock's Tara—on a smaller scale. No matter what furniture she chooses to include, Betsy Bradley sets the style with southern hospitality. The guest rooms are beautifully appointed with reproductions of Charleston rice-carved four-posters. The rest of the furniture resembles the eclectic mix of most Charleston homes: Empire, Queen Anne, Chippendale, and comfortable modern couches by the central fireplace in the living room, where guests relax after skiing or touring Woodstock.

A close friend of President Lincoln's once said, "The good people of Woodstock have less incentive than others to yearn for heaven." The Ottauquechee River rushes through, and four Paul Revere bells ring throughout the day. Woodstock even has its own covered bridge near the edge of the village green. This is a "safe" town where the police report lists more "domestic complaints" than "burglaries" (there were five of the latter in 1985).

Woodstock, which many people consider to be the prettiest village in Vermont, owes great thanks to the Laurence Rockefellers, who acted as silent benefactors for the town's up-scale renovation. With their assistance, gentrified shops with picture-perfect displays moved into the restored brick and clapboard buildings along the town's two main streets. A new cosmopolitan finesse shines on the bustling village.

The Charleston House is itself a part of this process. The Bradleys rebuilt the house to National Register specifications. One guest certainly appreciates the Bradleys' characteristic care: "I've stayed in hundreds of places like this, and this is the nicest I've found."

THE CHARLESTON HOUSE, 21 Pleasant Street, Woodstock, VT 05091; (802) 457-3843; Laird and Betsy Bradley, hosts. Some Spanish spoken. Open year-round except from mid-April to late May and two weeks in late fall. Seven guest rooms, all with private baths. Rates: $74 to $84, with full breakfast at table or continental breakfast in bed. Children 6 years and older welcome; no pets; no cigar smoking; Visa/MasterCard. A number of good restaurants are in the area. Shops, art galleries, antiques stores, summer theater. Bicycles provided. Alpine skiing, tennis, 18-hole Robert Trent Jones golf course, town pool nearby.

DIRECTIONS: from Rte. 89 get off at exit 1, the Woodstock-Rutland-Rte. 4 exit. Turn east on Rte. 4 and continue 10 miles into town. The inn is on Rte. 4, just east of the main intersection.

WHETSTONE INN

"The nicest inn in New England"

Jean and Harry Boardman moved to southern Vermont from southern California where Harry was secretary general for the Council for Biology and Human Affairs at the Salk Institute and where Jean edited a linguistics journal. Over the years Harry had stayed at this historic inn while in the area to give seminars on humanist subjects. And though neither he nor Jean had ever given thought to becoming innkeepers, six months after discovering that this 1786 tavern was for sale, the Boardmans were running the Whetstone Inn.

Marlboro is the classic New England village, consisting of a church, a post office, and an inn.

Warmhearted, intellectually stimulating, and decorated in a no-frills, comfortable style, the Whetstone elicits spontaneous testimonials. Rosy-cheeked from an afternoon of cross-country skiing, one thoroughly satisfied guest burst forth with unrestrained enthusiasm: "Do you want to know about this place? It's the epitome, the absolutely nicest inn in New England. Harry and Jean make it what it is. Jean is just the best chef. You can't believe what her cooking is like. . ."

Jean's cooking is, indeed, renowned, from her masterful handling of breakfast foods to the dinners she creates several times a week. Fortunate patrons might dine on homemade soup; leg of lamb with plum sauce; filet of beef or veal with white wine sauce; fresh salad; and, for dessert, a pie shell filled with chocolate mousse, or, the all-time favorite, apple cheddar cheese pie.

Tiny Marlboro is a classic, picture postcard village as well as a year-round resort. Summer brings many joys including the seven-week Marlboro Music Festival, a feast of chamber music with Rudolph Serkin as artistic director. Luminaries from the world of music, from Avery Fisher to Jean Pierre Rampal, might be table partners at one of Jean's dinners. Fall color is brilliant, and the loveliness of the flowers and vivid greens of spring beggars description. During the winter season the Whetstone offers excellent cross-country skiing on its eleven acres of hills and meadows, while downhill skiing is found a short drive away.

A "pre-Murphy" bed.

Left, heading for the cross-country ski trails.

WHETSTONE INN, Marlboro, VT 05344; (802) 254-2500; Jean and Harry Boardman, Hosts. French and some German spoken. Post-and-beam construction inn, built as a tavern around 1786. Open year-round. Eleven guest rooms, some with kitchenettes, some that accommodate four; shared and private baths. Rates: $25 singles, $45 to $60 doubles; $2 infant, $6 child, $10 third adult (15 and above). Hearty breakfast served; variety of good restaurants in area. Pets discouraged; checks accepted; Downhill and cross-country skiing, hiking, Marlboro Music Festival.

DIRECTIONS: drive 8 miles west from Brattleboro, Vt., on Rte. 9. Marlboro is ¼ mile off Rte. 9.

1811 HOUSE

A classic inn;
a classic village

This is not just another inn. The groomed and elegant 1811 House is impeccable inside and out. When Mary and Jack Hirst found this historic building, ideally situated next to the classic New England spired church on the equally classic Manchester village green, it was in need of complete renovation. They began by removing aluminum siding that encased the structure and hiring eight men to remove two centuries of paint. It took workers ten full weeks to uncover the original wood. Then the Federal capitals and moldings began to fall apart. So the Hirsts copied all of the embellishments and reinstated identical decorative moldings. Finally, the "two-over-two" Victorian cylinder glass windows were replaced by colonial-style twelve-pane glass. Jack didn't rest until each pane was filled with irregular antique glass.

The Hirsts tackled the interior with the same dedication and energy, painstakingly restoring original detail and adding private baths for each

A second floor guest room.
Another view of the inn can be seen on page 2,
facing the title page.

of the ten bedrooms. In the center of the building they created an English pub, in honor of Mary's homeland, complete with dartboard and working fireplace.

All of the rooms in the house are simple and lovely. The first-floor parlors and dining room are furnished from Mary's collection of fine English antiques, crystal, and paintings of country scenes. Each bedroom has its own color scheme and personality.

Britain inspires American inns, and Mary's authentic English breakfast shows us one reason why. Guests might be treated to kippers, sautéed chicken livers, or sole meunière; grilled tomatoes; sautéed apples and mushrooms, in addition to eggs, bacon, fried bread, and fresh-squeezed orange juice, all served on fine china and crystal.

1811 HOUSE, Manchester Village, VT 05254; (802) 362-1811; Mary and Jack Hirst, Pat and Jeremy David, hosts. Excellent example of Federal architecture, which was long a famous summer resort in the 1800s. Open year-round. Ten guest rooms, private baths. Rates: $65 to $105 double. Full English-style breakfast. No children under sixteen; no pets; major credit cards. Excellent dining in the area and occasional dinners served on premises for guests. Hiking, fishing, tennis, golf, swimming, antiquing, winter skiing.

DIRECTIONS: from Bennington, Vt., drive north on historic Rte. 7A. Inn is in Manchester Village on the green, next to the Congregational Church (with spire).

An unusual French fashion plate.

BEAUCHAMP
PLACE
Country Inn
Bed & Breakfast

VACANCY

East guest room has its own personality.

BEAUCHAMP PLACE

Anglophiles with exquisite taste

Roy and Georgia Beauchamp lived in England for fifteen years before they retired to the sophisticated, tidy village of Brandon. In planning, this astonishingly beautiful inn, they decided to adopt the amenities of Europe, adding touches characteristic of America's unique style of relaxation. In keeping with the style of this mansard-roofed manor house, Georgia chose wallpaper from the Victorian Historical Society Book and ordered new embossed tin ceilings for the third floor. Each of the eight bedrooms is furnished with Victorian and Empire pieces, many of which came from former Vermont estates. Down duvets, individually controlled heat, and plush, color-coordinated towels afford individual comfort.

A veritable museum collection of furniture and decorative art dwells in the downstairs common rooms: a burled walnut sideboard that survived the bombing in World War II, a 1765 Branson, Hull grandfather moon clock, Battersea Halcyon Days enamel boxes, a Royal Crown Darby collection, and soft, pink Venetian glass from Murano to name a few.

Anglophiles at heart, the Beauchamps became increasingly interested in genealogy when they lived abroad. Georgia researched church records in Britain, tracing her ancestors, who include two of the original Jamestown settlers, a poet laureate buried in Westminster Abbey and a dissenter buried in the Tower of London. Roy's lineage is equally impressive. His family came from Normandy with William the Conqueror in 1066. A recent relative was the keeper of the seal of Maryland, and first secretary of that state, in 1665.

BEAUCHAMP PLACE, Rte. 7, 31 Franklin Street, Brandon, VT 05733; (802) 247-3905; Roy and Georgia Beauchamp, innkeepers. Open all year. Eight rooms share four baths. Rates: $70 to $85; includes continental breakfast featuring fruit and freshly baked breads. Not suggested for children under sixteen; no pets; no smoking; American Express/MasterCard/Visa. Golf, tennis, skiing, watersports, croquet, sleigh rides; antiquing. Near to Middlebury College.

MASSACHUSETTS

NORTHFIELD COUNTRY HOUSE

A well-kept secret revealed

Hidden in the hills of the beautiful Connecticut River Valley, Northfield Country House is one of those special places that visitors hope to keep a secret, all to themselves.

The aura of romance begins as you wind your way up the drive. Trees suddenly part to reveal a gracefully proportioned English manor house built in 1901 by a wealthy Boston shipbuilder who had an eye for beauty and the purse to pursue it. He insisted upon the finest handcarved cherry wainscoting, mantels, and doors; a broad staircase; leaded glass windows; and a twelve-foot stone hearth in which is embedded the message, "Love Warms The Heart As Fire The Hearth."

Andrea Dale's country house has been decorated with an eye to combining design and color into an art form. The living room with its stone hearth and three plush and generous couches invites quiet relaxation and easy conversation.

The house offers the comforts of home plus special extras—pretty sitting areas in all of the guest rooms, rich Bokara and Herziz carpets to cushion the foot. A romantic hideaway with working fireplace, velvet settee, and thick comforter on an antique bed feels rich and warm; another blue and white chamber complete with brass and iron bedstead and white wicker armchair is crisp, fresh, and old-fashioned.

Breakfast, which is served on the porch in the summer and in the cherry-paneled dining room when the weather is wet or cold, is simply splendid, with popovers and cheese and mushroom omelcts the popular fare. *Prix fixe* dinners are offered several times a week.

NORTHFIELD COUNTRY HOUSE, School St., Northfield, MA 01360; (413) 498-2692; Andrea Dale, owner. English manor house set on 16 acres. Open year-round. Seven guest rooms, shared baths. Rates: $35 to $70. Full breakfast served daily, five-course dinner served Thurs.-Sat. Children 10 and over; no pets; Visa/MasterCard; checks accepted.

DIRECTIONS: take I-91 to Exit 28A. Follow Rte. 10 north to Northfield Center. School St. is in center of town, at the firehouse. Turn at firehouse and drive 9/10 of a mile. Inn driveway is on right. *Note:* Since street becomes narrow dirt road, driving in snowy or wet conditions can be difficult. Please have good tires!

Left, the dining room set for breakfast, with Janice's delicious Swiss cereal. Above, each guest room has its own character.

Hosts Brad Wagstaff and Leslie Miller.

THE OLD INN ON THE GREEN

A sleepy village floodlit at night

Brad Wagstaff bought this charming eighteenth-century inn as a restoration project a half-dozen years ago. Leslie Miller came to the Berkshires to train as a baker, rented a room in the partially renovated inn, and fell in love with Brad and the Berkshires.

The New Marlborough green is pastoral and idyllic, a sleepy village whose cluster of Greek Revival relics—most especially the Town Meeting House, dramatically floodlit at night—reflects a burst of commerce long since past. A short walk along the town's quiet main road takes strollers past Brad's flock of sheep and large herd of dairy cattle. Wander down the lane just next to the inn to discover some of the most spectacular scenery in the Berkshire Mountains.

The inn, which is being meticulously restored to its original glory, is casual and wonderfully atmospheric. Bedrooms are furnished with a combination of classic antiques and funky art deco and forties accoutrements. The second-floor balcony was made for a leisurely morning of reading, coffee drinking, or just watching the sun move higher in the sky.

The inn features a formal dinner each Friday and Saturday night, served in the three downstairs dining rooms. With the aid of a talented local chef, Leslie and Brad offer a five-course *prix fixe* menu that changes with the seasons and unfolds beautifully in the soft glow of candlelight and firelight.

THE OLD INN ON THE GREEN, New Marlborough, MA 01230; (413) 229-7924; Leslie Miller and Brad Wagstaff, hosts. Spanish spoken by Leslie. Built in 1760 as an inn, this Greek Revival gem also once served as tavern, stagecoach stop, general store, and post office. Open weekends year-round. Five guest rooms; private and shared baths. Rates: $60 to $75 per room. Continental breakfast. No pets; checks accepted; no credit cards. Summer theater nearby; excellent dining in area.

DIRECTIONS: from New York City, take Taconic Pkwy. to Rte. 23 exit. Take 23 through Great Barrington and go east toward Monterrey. Turn right on Rte. 57 before Monterry and follow for 5.7 miles. From Boston, take Mass. Tnpke. to Lee exit. Take Rte. 7 through Stockbridge to Rte. 23, and 23 toward Monterrey, following directions above.

CORNELL HOUSE

Cabaret conviviality still echoes here

New owners Jack and Vicki D'Elia have completely renovated the stately Cornell House. A speakeasy during Prohibition, this graceful Queen Anne Victorian still echoes its colorful past.

Facing the four-hundred-acre Kennedy Park, open to the public year-round, the communal breakfast parlor with floor-to-ceiling windows is a favorite gathering spot. A deck with tables and colorful umbrellas can be glimpsed from the dining table, and guests are welcome to eat breakfast al fresco, when the weather permits. In the evening, dining tables transform into game tables and conversation often continues into the wee hours.

Behind the main house is Hill House, a two-story converted barn, especially charming in warm months when shuttered windows are accented with flowering window boxes. Newly developed into four luxury apartments, each unit has its own bedroom, living room, and dining room and features a private deck, galley kitchen, Jacuzzi, fireplace, and air conditioning.

Here, in a location central to both busy Lenox Center and Tanglewood, the D'Elias go all out for their guests, making reservations, supplying schedules, providing knowing suggestions, finding hiking trails, helping them on their way, and, finally, welcoming them back home with an inexhaustable supply of wine and cheese.

CORNELL HOUSE. 197 Pittsfield Rd., Lenox, MA 01240; (413) 637-0562; Jack and Vicki D'Elia, hosts. Charming inn, circa 1888, Victorian-style. Open year-round. Nine guest rooms in main house, four luxury suites in "Hill House," all with private baths. Three night minimum in season. Rates: $275 for two people for three nights, $55 per night during week, $850 per week for suite. Rates include light breakfast; excellent dining nearby. No children in main house; no pets; Visa/MasterCard. The Berkshires offer year-round recreation, cultural events, historic events, antiques.

DIRECTIONS: from New York City, take the Taconic Pkwy. to Rte. 23 exit. Take 23E through Great Barrington to Rte. 7. Take Rte. 7 to Rte. 7A (Lenox Centre) and turn left. Drive through Lenox and up hill to inn on left, just past church. From Mass. Turnpike, take Lee exit 2. Turn right onto Rte. 20W and drive through Lee. Turn left onto Rte. 183 and proceed to Lenox Centre.

BULLFROG BED & BREAKFAST

For weary travelers

In the heart of Mohawk Trail and sugar maple country, adventurous visitors will find the Bullfrog Bed and Breakfast. Moses and Lucille Thibault, converted their children's rooms into plain, uncluttered nooks for weary travelers. Instead of age-old antiques and cunningly designed handcrafts, the Thibaults emphasize true hospitality and good country cooking.

Breakfast around the long table is a lush affair in any season because Lucille's nurtured houseplants hang at every level along the multi-paned windowed wall. Summer guests can hear the chorus of frogs in the pond out back and might even catch a glimpse of the Thibault's gray horse trotting behind the house.

If you arrive in late winter or early spring as the thaw sets in, Moses may be out sugaring, boiling down the sap collected from their "sugar orchard" next door.

BULLFROG BED AND BREAKFAST, Box 210, Star Route, Ashfield, MA 01330; (413) 628-4493; Lucille and Moses Thibault, hosts. Open year-round except Christmas. Some French spoken. Two guest rooms share one bath; one guest room has an adjoining bath; honeymoon cottage down the road. Rates: $25, single; $35 to $40, double; includes hearty breakfast. Children welcome; no pets; no smoking preferred; no credit cards. Spring-fed pond has good swimming; Mohawk Trail; Old Deerfield museums; Hoosac Tunnel Museum; antiquing.

DIRECTIONS: from Rte. 91, take exit 24 (S. Deerfield) to 116W through Conway. Begin watching for green mile markers. At approximately mile 42½, the farmhouse is on the right (by Murray Rd.)

Breakfast is cooked on this wood stove.

MERRELL TAVERN INN

Fine antiques in a stagecoach inn

Catering to travelers since the 1800s, the old Merrell Tavern has been painstakingly restored to its former glory by Charles and Faith Reynolds. It is now elegantly furnished with fine Sheraton and Heppelwhite antiques the Reynolds have collected over twenty-five years. Canopied, four-poster, and pencil-post bedsteads with deluxe mattresses, sought out for their exquisite comfort, ensure a pleasurable night's sleep. In the morning guests gather in the tavern for breakfast, which may feature Charles' special omelets, pancakes, and sausages, or perhaps a new find from a cookbook. A visit will reveal more treasures; there is not space here to do them justice.

MERRELL TAVERN INN, Rte. 102, South Lee., MA 01260; (413) 243-1794; Charles and Faith Reynolds, hosts. Closed Christmas Eve and Day. Seven guest rooms in inn proper, one in old summer kitchen, one in old smokehouse; fireplaces in three rooms, all with private baths. Rates: $40 to $100 double, according to season and amenities, weekend packages available. All rates include full breakfast. No pets; major credit cards.

DIRECTIONS: exit Mass. Turnpike at Lee (exit 2) and follow Rte. 102 three miles toward Stockbridge.

79

In its day, this was considered the Rolls Royce of stoves; the Glenwood Parlor Stove, with cherubs, c. 1908.

Cod, where the Heberts used to live, are equally beautiful. Fresh flowers and a basket of toiletries await every guest. Terrycloth robes hang in closets for those who must share a bath. Down comforters or Linda's handmade quilts cover each bed.

Linda's artistry is visible throughout the house. Her Star of Bethlehem wall quilt won first prize at the Barnstable (Mass.) County Fair, and since moving to Ashfield she placed second as Homemaker of the Year in Franklin County, making top-quality preserves and canned goods.

Linda's skills extend to the kitchen, where her German apple pancake reigns supreme at breakfast. To top it all off, Roger and Linda offer an elegant, delectable dinner to guests only.

ASHFIELD INN, Main St., P.O. Box 129, Ashfield, MA 01330; (413) 628-4571; Roger and Linda Hebert, innkeepers. Open all year. Rates: $70 for two, including an elegant breakfast. Dinner featuring fresh seasonal foods is an additional $16 per person. Four guest rooms share two baths; the Chatham Room has a private bathroom with shower. Golf, swimming or skating and ice fishing on the lake. Dining in Northampton and Greenfield. Smoking allowed in the living room only; no pets; some facilities for children are available; American Express/MasterCard/Visa accepted.

DIRECTIONS: from points south, take Rte. 91N to Deerfield (exit 24) to Rtes. 5 and 10N one mile, turn left onto 116N and continue 17 miles to Ashfield Center. From the west, take Rte. 20 to Pittsfield, 9E to Goshen, and 112 to Ashfield Center.

ASHFIELD INN

A romantic masterpiece

Cleome, foxglove, evening primrose, and lunaria recall ancient potions to remedy the lovelorn. Ashfield Inn's summer garden blooms in resplendent color with these perennials. Roger and Linda Hebert bought this stately Georgian mansion after it had been on the market for five years. Uncared for and in great disrepair, the old manor house was nearly lost. This talented couple have transformed the building into a romantic masterpiece.

The front door opens into a great hall with a Glenwood wood stove with cherubs, the "Rolls-Royce of parlor stoves in 1908," says Roger. The living room, to the right, focuses on the fireplace, bounded on either side by double French doors. The mantel defines Georgian elegance, as do the interior archways and moldings of the whole inn.

The bedrooms, each named for a town on Cape

This room is named Wianno.

HAUS ANDREAS

Bed and breakfast with amenities

Haus Andreas; a full-service bed and breakfast, is a vacation in itself where good food and entertainment are the focus. Host Gerhard Schmid, an internationally acclaimed chef who has cooked for President Kennedy, the Queen of England, and the Shah of Iran, and his wife Lilliane also

own and operate the Gateways Inn, a sister lodging in nearby Lenox, that boasts a fine restaurant overflowing with Gerhard's good food. Guests at Haus Andreas—named for the Schmid's son, receive preferred seats in the Gateways dining room.

Continental breakfast at the house is elegant, with white linen, china, silver, and a view that is truly inspiring—manicured lawns, birch trees, the orchards, and the mountains.

The formal, well-appointed bedrooms are clean and spare, with fussiness and embellishments kept to a minimum. Antiques in such a setting assume center spotlight.

Outdoors, volleyball, tennis, croquet, and badminton keep many guests busy on the property. The nine-hole golf course across the street attracts many visitors, and bicycles (including a tandem) are available to guests who want to stray a little farther.

HAUS ANDREAS, RR 1, Box 605-B, Stockbridge Road, Lee, MA 01238; (413) 243-3298; Gerhard and Lilliane Schmid, innkeepers. Six guest rooms, all with private baths, two with fireplaces; suite available. Rates: weekends in summer range from $80 to $145; midweek, $55 to $90; additional person is approximately $15; use of fireplace in season is $8. A $3.50 charge is added to the bill for the maids. No pets; no children under ten. No out-of-state checks; Visa/MasterCard. Fine dining throughout the area.

DIRECTIONS: call for specific directions.

Breakfast is served in the main living room.

THE TURNING POINT

Once frequented by Daniel Webster

The acquisition of an old stagecoach stop was a turning point for Shirley and Irv Yost. Situated at the turning point in the road, the inn reflects their commitment to a new lifestyle that includes a growing passion for good food.

Breakfast is worth the trip in itself. As Shirley explains, "During college our children changed to vegetarian diets, and this sparked our interest. After several years of experimenting with this diet, one thing led to another, and before we knew it we opened a bed and breakfast devoted to good, delicious food. A friend of ours has suggested that we bill ourselves as *Breakfast and Bed.*"

The focus of each breakfast is whole grains, though the Yosts can cater to wheat-free and other special diets. An average meal might include feather-light whole wheat-and-bran pancakes served with maple syrup, hot baked fruits or fresh fruit salad, eggs, juice, and grain coffee, herbal tea, and the more common brews. Irv often makes a frittata flavored with a mixture of summer vegetables, a robust concoction that he has earlier frozen to provide a cure for the winter blahs. To fill out each abundant meal, Shirley bakes whole grain fruit breads, which she serves with apple butter or natural peanut butter. The Yosts make every effort to offer foods that contain no preservatives or chemicals.

A stay at the Turning Point, which is furnished with an eclectic mix of antiques and well-loved pieces from their home, is casual, comfortable, and very satisfying.

THE TURNING POINT, Rte. 23 and Lake Buel Rd., RD-2 Box 140, Great Barrington, MA 01230; (413) 528-4777; Irv and Shirley Yost, hosts. Federal style older section of house was once tavern-inn frequented by Daniel Webster. Open all year, with occasional off-season closings. Seven guest rooms, most sharing baths. Rates: $40 to $45 single, $55 to $65 double. Includes elaborate vegetarian breakfast; special diets accommodated. Afternoon tea. Wide range of good dining nearby. Children welcome; no pets; no smoking; no credit cards. Prime Berkshire location offers year-round recreation, sight-seeing, antiquing.

DIRECTIONS: from NYC, take Taconic Pkwy. to Rte. 23. Inn is 21 miles east on Rte. 23 (through Great Barrington) at Lake Buel Rd. From Boston, take Mass. Turnpike to Lee exit (2) onto Rte. 102 W, through Stockbridge to Rte. 750. Follow to Rte. 23, turn left; 2½ miles to inn.

THE COLONEL EBENEZER CRAFTS INN

Owned by the Publick House

Built in 1786 by David Fiske, Esq., The Colonel Ebenezer Crafts Inn is a contemporary of its famous neighbor, Old Sturbridge Village. The inn is well-situated atop Fiske Hill, along a quiet road where peace reigns supreme, and it is blessed with landscaped grounds capacious enough for a large swimming pool, as well as ongoing badminton, croquet, and frisbee tournaments. The house is a large, eight-bedroom colonial-that-grew, filled with a compatible collection of antiques and period reproductions. The living room combines the elegance of a baby grand piano, a massive antique oriental area rug, and formal colonial moldings with the comforts of a television/library alcove and bright, plant-filled sunroom. Each cozy bedroom is stocked with a supply of fresh fruits and cookies, terrycloth robes, extra pillows, and a pot of jam to take home as a memento.

At breakfast, guests fall heir to the bounty of the bakery of the Publick House, Craft's big sister inn, with sinfully delicious, fre... sticky buns, spicy pumpkin or blue... or old-fashioned cornbread sticks. Th... be taken in the casual first-floor parlor o... breakfast tray in bed. For a more substantial... the Publick House dining room, one mile down the road, offers a classic version of New England red flannel hash, apple pie with cheddar cheese, a variety of egg dishes, and celestial pancakes served with hot maple syrup. Known for its high-quality foods and generous portions, the Publick House is a good choice for afternoon and evening meals as well.

THE COLONEL EBENEZER CRAFTS INN, c/o Publick House, On the Common, Sturbridge, MA 01566; (617) 347-3313; Patricia and Henri Bibeau, hosts. Federal style house open all year. Eight guest rooms, including two suites, all with private baths; rollaways and cribs available. Room rates $75 to $87 double, according to season and amenities; Cottage Suite $100 to $109, varying seasonally; including light breakfast featuring home-baked breads. Excellent dining nearby. Children welcome; no pets; major credit cards. Old Sturbridge Village nearby brings pre-Revolutionary America to life.

DIRECTIONS: from Albany or Boston, take Mass. Turnpike to Exit 9. Bear left (do not go toward Old Sturbridge Village) to Publick House on Rte. 131. Inquire within for directions. From Hartford, take I-84 East to Sturbridge. Take Exit 3. Bear right, then turn left and follow road to back entrance of Publick House. Inquire within for directions to inn.

The building on the right contains a private suite, and the grounds keep the children occupied.

Hostess Marilyn Mudry makes all the quilts.

HAWTHORNE INN

Steeped in American history

Concord, Massachusetts, is among those rare geographical points that seem to emit a force that attracts, inspires, and provokes man to action. The "shot heard round the world" sounded at Old North Bridge and triggered the Revolutionary War. Nearby Walden Pond moved Henry David Thoreau to record profound observations on nature and mankind. Nathaniel Hawthorne, Ralph Waldo Emerson, and the Alcotts made their homes in Concord, nurtured by its ineffable energy.

The Hawthorne Inn offers guests the opportunity to discover Concord and perhaps to experience the force that so inspired America's Transcendentalists. Originally owned by Hawthorne himself, the property has a fascinating history. Good friend Bronson Alcott constructed a Bath House on the land just behind the inn and, using "sylvan architecture," created other elaborate structures made from forest finds. The Bath House was to be his grandest building, the magnetic point of all his other artworks. Though the building no longer stands, trees planted by these famous neighbors bear silent testimony to its earlier presence. Across from the inn sits Hawthorne's home "Wayside." Grapevine Cottage, where the Concord grape was developed, is another close neighbor.

In the mid-1970s artist Gregory Burch was attracted to Concord and to this house, which was large enough to contain his painting and sculpture studio as well as rooms for wayfarers. He and his wife Marilyn offer guests the comforts of an impeccably maintained and antiques-filled home. Gregory's soapstone bas-relief carvings and energetic paintings, and Marilyn's beautifully designed quilts contribute, along with books of poetry and art, and Mayan and Inca artifacts, to make the Hawthorne Inn a very stimulating haven.

HAWTHORNE INN , 462 Lexington Rd., Concord MA 01742; (617) 369-5610; Gregory Burch and Marilyn Mudry, hosts. Charming inn on site steeped in American history. Open all year. Seven guest rooms, private and shared baths. Rates: $70 single, $90 double, $20 third person. Continental breakfast. No credit cards; no pets. Wide variety of restaurants within 10-minute drive. Equally wide variety of sports and spots of interest in this scenic country.

DIRECTIONS: from Rte. 128–95, take Exit 45 west for 3½ miles. Bear right at the single blinking light. Inn is one mile on left, across from "Wayside" (Hawthorne and Alcott home).

CHARLES HINCKLEY HOUSE

Where no detail is overlooked

"A small, intimate country inn where great expectations are quietly met." The Charles Hinckley House's brochure tells the truth. The house defines elegant simplicity. Hosts Miya and Les Patrick are consummate professionals. Their goal is to indulge each guest with exquisite perfection.

Situated on the Olde Kings Highway in a historic district, the Federal Colonial house bespeaks warmth, relaxation, and romance. Every room boasts a working fireplace, private bath, and period furnishings that blend well with the rich plums and blues of the decor.

No details are overlooked. Miya's wildflower garden provides fresh bouquets to complement the exotic blooms she specially orders in. Her breakfast is a succulent testament to her aesthetic sense; choosing a combination of tropical and local fruits, she presents a platter so pleasing that it was featured in full color in *Country Living* magazine. Homemade *creme fraiche* is available

Hosts Miya and Les Patrick.

as an alternative to cream or milk, and handmade chocolates accompany the turn-down service. Flannel sheets in winter and cotton ones in summer dress the beds, with covers of down comforters or handcrafted quilts which add just the right amount of coziness. Guests also enjoy scented soaps, toiletries, thick-piled cotton bath sheets.

Evenings are casual, with impromptu gatherings in the living room; however, privacy is as easily achievable. Honeymooners can expect a bottle of champagne and breakfast in bed, if they wish.

Miya and Les, as young as they are, have been pampering people for years—first at The Inn at Phillips Mill in New Hope, Pennsylvania, then at Graywillow, also on the Cape—but never as well as they do now. A stay here will surely prove their expertise.

CHARLES HINCKLEY HOUSE, Box 723, Barnstable Village, MA 02630; (617) 362-9924; Les and Miya Patrick, innkeepers. Open year round. Rates: $85 to $125 with full breakfast. Four guest rooms, all with private baths and working fireplaces. Children over 12 welcome; no pets; no smoking.

DIRECTIONS: from Rte. 3 take Rte. 6 to exit 6. At the end of the ramp, turn left. Turn right onto 6A at the stop sign (½ mile down the road). Go ½ mile more, and the house is on a slight rise to the left.

Very special breakfasts.

BEECHWOOD

A classic Cape Cod getaway cottage

Turning onto the Old Kings Highway, strains of Patti Page singing "Old Cape Cod" suddenly come to mind. The road to Beechwood meanders along classic sand dunes, past traditional clapboard-and-shingle cottages partially obscured by graceful, weathered trees. Amidst all this beauty, Beechwood is an especially romantic house, a Victorian cottage colored in the softest shades of jade green, butter yellow, and muted brick. Shaded by century-old copper beech trees, Beechwood is a classic Cape Cod getaway.

Myles and Sandy Corey chose this Greek Revival-Queen Anne-Eastlake hybrid after years of dreaming about owning a home on the Cape; "our nest in the world." Sweethearts since high school, the Coreys' ongoing romance suffuses the house with good vibrations. Myles, a traditional portrait and landscape artist, maintains his studio here and guests are invited to see him at work.

Both Myles and Sandy are gifted cooks and dinner is available upon request. Typical fare might include stuffed mussels, home[...] England clam chowder, boiled succulent [...] potato, vegetables, and anything from [...] torte to an elegant chocolate soufflé for des[...]

One favorite bedroom, often requested by honeymooners, contains a four-poster bed of such grand proportions, that many guests need a booster stool to clamber up and under the covers. Another bedroom is a pristine jewel: lace-edged white sheets and down comforter, a white wicker rocker, and lace curtains accent a shiny brass bed, marble fireplace and a ruby velvet rocking chair. In the high, peaked garret another room is found. Through a half-moon window, guests can gaze past the treetops to the neighboring dunes and water.

Barnstable is a quiet village centrally located to all points in the Cape. Comprised of private residences and containing an assortment of fine antiques shops, it is a wonderful place to catch the magical mood of Cape Cod—the stuff about which songs are written.

BEECHWOOD, 2839 Main St., Barnstable Village, MA 02630; (617) 362-6618; Myles and Sandy Corey, hosts. Some French spoken. Victorian shingled house with large porch and tinted windows. Open all year. Six distinctive guest rooms, two with fireplaces, all private baths. Rates $75 to $105 per room, including hearty, full breakfast. Afternoon tea. Excellent seafood dining in area. No children; no pets; no smoking; Visa/MasterCard/American Express. Cape Cod offers dunes, beaches, boating, antiques.

Left, high tea by the hearth.

The Capt. Harding Room has a fireplace and a bay window.

CAPTAIN DEXTER HOUSE

Island living at its best

Three blocks from the ferry, and the first home in the historic residential district of Vineyard Haven, The Captain Dexter House stands as a model of elegance, comfort, and convenience. Guests here can experience island living at its best—without billboards, fast-food franchises, not even stoplights—only picturesque seaside villages, quiet harbors, and glorious white sand beaches.

Martha's Vineyard is world-renowned for its natural beauty as well as its celebrities. The flat, straight southern shore provides miles of glacially carved, wave-dashed beach. The gentle curves on the island's other two sides lead into the calmer waters of Nantucket Sound to the east and Vineyard Sound to the west. North and center lies the year-round town which Lara and Beyer Parker now call home.

Beyer likes to describe his old sea captain's house as a "Federalized Victorian" with a peaked roof, bay windows, and side porch, but the interior recalls colonial times. A Williamsburg-style reproduction table assumes center stage in the dining room, flanked by Queen Anne-style chairs and beyond by a Sheraton breakfront and a Scottish grandfather clock that dates back to 1812. The far wall hosts two portraits painted in 1843, the same year that the house was built.

The eight well-kept guest rooms reflect the consideration the Parkers put into the common rooms. Antiques and contemporary furnishings provide a pleasing mix that suits modern demands for comfort and charm.

THE CAPTAIN DEXTER HOUSE, Box 2457, 100 Main Street, Vineyard Haven, Martha's Vineyard, MA 02568; (617) 693-6564; Lara and Beyer Parker, hosts. Open all year. Eight guest rooms, all with private baths, two with working fireplaces. Rates: $80 to $110 in season; $50 to $85 off-season; $15 for an additional person. Children over eleven are welcome; no pets; smoking in guest rooms only; MasterCard/Visa. Guest refrigerator, beach towels, locked garage for bicycles. Watersports; horseback riding; summer theater; good restaurants nearby.

DIRECTIONS: Car reservations to and from Woods Hole should be made well in advance. Write or call the Parkers.

WINDAMAR HOUSE

Provincetown mix of antiques and art

At the tip of a twenty-five mile arc of beaches and windswept sand dunes, Provincetown, the terminus of Cape Cod, is a year-round resort of exceptional beauty. Summertime ushers in the carnival season. Two main thoroughfares, lined with art galleries, shops, museums, and restaurants, teem with tourists and sun worshippers. The contemplative beauty of the spring and fall attracts naturalists and artists. In winter, uncluttered by people and protected from Arctic temperatures by ocean currents, this spectacular landscape reveals its basic lines.

In any season Windamar House is a fine place to stay. Bette Adams' Cape colonial house sits in a quiet residential pocket just "this side" of Provincetown's commercial district. Windamar has a picket-fenced front yard, gardens, a terraced backyard filled with lawn furniture, and, most importantly, a private parking lot. In a town that can't expand geographically, all of the above are at a premium.

A guest suite.

The stairway leading to the second-floor guest rooms.

Inside, the second-floor bedrooms range from a tiny cubbyhole to a suite with cathedral ceiling and a wall of glass. Besides single rooms, two fully equipped apartments are available for longer stays. Original art fills all available walls throughout the house, and bedrooms are an eclectic mix of antiques and comfortable period pieces.

Though Bette is always about, making sure the coffee pot is filled in the morning and seeing to the needs of her guests, she is not an intrusive presence. Free to barbecue in the backyard or sit for hours in the lounge (complete with "no-cook" kitchen), guests settle in and make themselves at home.

WINDAMAR HOUSE, 568 Commercial St., Provincetown, MA 02657; (617) 487-0599; Bette Adams, hostess. Some French spoken. Two houses joined together in the quiet east end of Provincetown. Open all year. Six guest rooms, sharing baths, and two fully equipped apartments. Rates $32 to $65 main house, according to season and room; apartments $50 per night off season, two-night minimum, $395 per week in season; rates include continental breakfast for rooms only. Excellent dining nearby. No children; no pets; no credit cards. Provincetown offers incomparable natural setting, year-round recreation, bird-watching, whale-watching.

DIRECTIONS: Take Cape Hwy. (Rte. 6) to Provincetown. Take first exit to water and turn right on 6A. At 'V' in road bear left onto Commercial St. Windamar House is ¼ mile ahead on right. Boats and flights available from Boston.

RHODE ISLAND

THE OLD DENNIS HOUSE

Bed and breakfast in Newport

Newport is many things to many people, from sailing mecca to the site of architectural wonders, from peerless colonial structures to ostentatious turn-of-the-century palaces.

The oldest section of Newport, known as The Point, is a quiet neighborhood filled with vintage homes, many of which were built in the mid-1700s when Newport was a major port city second only to Boston. Though Newport never fully recovered from the crippling destruction of the British occupation in 1776, the charm of The Point survived. Situated on the oldest street in Newport, the Old Dennis House stands out among these gracious survivors. Built in 1740 by Captain John Dennis, it serves as rectory for St. John's Episcopal Church and is one of Newport's finest bed and breakfast establishments.

Reverend Henry G. Turnbull had been rector of St. John's for over twenty years when a bed and breakfast registry persuaded him to open the spacious third floor of the rectory to guests. Besides the pleasure of meeting interesting people and offering comfortable accommodations to weary wayfarers (certainly a work of mercy), upkeep of the rectory was erased from the parish budget!

Each guest room is simple and charming with lots of exposed brickwork, several working fireplaces, and an eclectic mix of antiques. Located several blocks from the hubbub of Thames Street and Brick Market Place, the Old Dennis House is convenient to the bustling waterfront but feels a world removed.

THE OLD DENNIS HOUSE, 59 Washington St., Newport, RI 02840; (401) 846-1324; Rev. Henry G. Turnbull, host. Five guest rooms plus luxury suite in adjacent building; all with private baths. Working fireplaces, air conditioning, TV. Open year-round. Rates: double $65 to $85 in summer, $50 to $60 in winter. Continental breakfast. Checks accepted.

DIRECTIONS: from Connecticut, cross Newport Bridge and take downtown Newport exit; 200 ft. off exit, turn right at light onto Van Zandt Ave. Go 3 blocks to Washington St. and turn left. Inn is about 7 blocks. From Boston, follow signs to Goat Island. At causeway to island, go 2 blocks north on Washington to corner of Poplar St.

St. John's Episcopal Church and the Rectory.

CLIFFSIDE INN

The grandeur of the Victorian age

Cliffside Inn captures the grandeur of the Victorian age with flowing curtains, bay windows, and commodious common rooms. This Second Empire summer cottage, which now stands among many beautiful houses in a peaceful residential district, once dominated the acreage. But even as times have changed, the luxury of the inn remains, as exemplified by the hallway floor's coat of arms, the last remnant of Cliffside's grand ballroom which burned down decades ago.

The ten guest rooms, all with private bath facilities, are imaginatively decorated. The coral and dark sea green of Miss Adele's Room is incorporated into a fireplace mantel that now functions as a headboard for the queen-sized bed. The Miss Beatrice Room, a favorite with newly-weds, is dressed in pinks and blues with bay windows and a Lincoln bed. Repeat visitors often ask for the light-filled Arbor Room situated off the porch. Its glass wall reminded one visitor of being in a botanical conservatory.

Cliffside has an unusual history. Built in 1880, the house served as a summer retreat for the governor of Maryland. Sixteen years later it became the site of a private preparatory school. The most famous denizen was Beatrice Pastorius Turner, who gained fame as a self-portrait artist and who painted the mother-daughter oil painting that hangs in the living room on the wall to the right of the piano. Her notoricty, however, came from her eccentricities. A recluse obsessed with youth, she walked into the town wearing Victorian clothes up until the 1940s.

Cliff Walk is about a ten-minute stroll away; the beach, even closer. All in all, Cliffside is a welcome addition to Newport's attractions.

CLIFFSIDE INN, 2 Seaview Avenue, Newport, RI 02840; (401) 847-1811; Kay Russell, innkeeper. Open May to October. Ten guest rooms plus an efficiency apartment, all with private baths. Rates: $54.50 to $76.30; slightly higher in season. The rate includes tax and a continental breakfast. Children over eleven welcome; no pets; cats on premises.

DIRECTIONS: from I-95, take Rte. 138 over the Newport Bridge. Take a right onto Americas Cup Ave. and bear left onto Memorial Blvd. Take a right onto Cliff Ave. The inn is on the left, at the corner of Sea View Ave.

Left, the Lincoln bed in the Miss Beatrice Room

First-floor formal parlor.

BRINLEY VICTORIAN INN

Unpretentious, well-tended, relaxed

On a quiet street off the beaten track, yet close to both the bustle of town and the mansions of Bellevue Avenue, the Brinley Victorian Inn is really two houses, a mansard-roofed Victorian frame and a smaller, adjoining counterpart. The parlor in the main house is formal and eye-pleasing, filled with Victorian settees, a rocker, and lace-draped tables, all in soft shades of green and cream. In the evening, guests congregate here, or in the game room at the rear of the house, comparing notes on the day's activities, preparing the next day's schedule, or relaxing over a game of cards. The overall atmosphere at the Brinley is unpretentious, friendly, well-tended, and relaxed.

The seventeen guest rooms are furnished with an easy mix of Victorian and contemporary pieces, and featured in each is one of owner Edwina Sebest's collection of antique miniature lamps and candlesticks. She and partner Amy Weintraub left high-powered jobs in Pittsburgh—Amy was a television writer and executive producer, Edwina a psychologist in private practice—to move to this city they both truly love. They operate a nursing home three blocks from the inn but are often at the Brinley to help out with chores and to visit with their guests.

THE BRINLEY VICTORIAN INN, 23 Brinley St., Newport, RI 02840; (401) 849-7645; Elizabeth Stouffer, host; Dr. Edwina Sebest and Amy Weintraub, owners. Open year-round; Seventeen guest rooms; seven with private baths. Two newly restored Victorian houses connected by walkway. Rates by room: winter, $55 to 75, summer, $65 to $95; $10 per extra person in room. Continental breakfast. No children under twelve; no pets; checks accepted. Extensive dining in area.

DIRECTIONS: from Newport/Jamestown bridge (Rte. 138), take downtown Newport exit. Go to third light and turn left onto Touro. At second light, turn left on Kay, and then right on Brinley. From north, take Rte. 114 into downtown. At movie theaters, bear left onto Touro and repeat above directions.

QUEEN ANNE INN

PHOENIX INN

Right in the center of Newport

The Queen Anne Inn captures the essence of unpretentious cordiality. Peg McCabe had the foresight to buy a well-located guest house right in the center of Newport.

Through plan and happenstance the quality of light in the Queen Anne is remarkable. A stained glass window lit from behind at night casts a glow resembling late afternoon sun into the hallway. The soft warmth from sunlight and from the many lamps suffuses through the lacy, pastel-hued, refined rooms, lending a restful mood to the entire inn.

Peg developed an interest in fixtures as well as lighting and takes pride in her choices. One of her favorite lamps sits on the table in the parlor—the base was a discovery at a salvage yard that deals with old estates. Peg decorated the fourteen guest rooms with the same steady hand, choosing fine antiques and accessories to adorn the four stories.

The Queen Anne is located on a quiet one-way street only two blocks from Newport's waterfront shops.

THE QUEEN ANNE INN, 16 Clarke Street, Newport, RI 02840; (401) 846-5676; Peg McCabe, innkeeper. Open April 1 through mid-November. Queen Anne Victorian that dates back to the 1890s. Fourteen rooms share seven baths. Rates: $30 to $60; generous and elegant continental breakfast included. Children welcome; no pets; Visa/MasterCard.

DIRECTIONS: from Touro Street take a left onto Clarke Street, a one-way street one block long. The inn is on your left.

A Stanford White original

Joyce and Dave Peterson are a joy to be around. It's the hosts' good humor that makes the Phoenix such a special place.

The shingle "cottage" is a trim Standford White original, rebuilt by architect Kenneth Murchison. He redesigned it to include separate small wings instead of one long hallway with rooms opening right and left. Each wing houses two cheerful bedrooms and one spotless shared bath. Guests who prefer more privacy can request the third-floor hideaway with its own bath.

"B-level tennis players are very welcome, as are fishermen," chuckles Dave. He and Joyce will even prepare early breakfasts for serious anglers—and it's a feast. Past menus have included peaches and cream French toast, lobster quiche, or boursin and broccoli omelets accompanied by apricot fan cake, oatmeal muffins, or Russian coffee cake. Fresh fruit, crisp bacon, and fresh-brewed mocha java with ground hazelnuts complete the meal.

PHOENIX INN, 29 Gibson Avenue, Narragansett, RI 02882; (401) 783-1918; Joyce and Dave Peterson, hosts. Open all year. Five guest rooms with shared and private baths; Rates: $45, single; $55, double. Full breakfast served. No pets; smoking permitted on the first floor only. Ocean swimming, tennis, golf, fishing; Theater-By-The-Sea close by.

DIRECTIONS: from Rte. 1 heading north, take a right onto S. Pier Rd. Take a right onto Gibson Ave. Look for the stone pillars on the right (Earles Ct. Rd. will be on the left). Take a right and follow the driveway to the Phoenix. There's no sign. From Rte. 1 heading south, take the right turn loop that leads to S. Pier Rd. going east.

CONNECTICUT

RED BROOK INN

A colonial gem near Mystic Seaport

Sitting in a California Victorian house filled with a lifetime's collection of Early American antiques, Ruth Keyes came to the conclusion that she would never feel altogether at home in the West. So when husband Vern Sasek suggested she find them a house in New England, she didn't miss a beat. Within six months Ruth and Vern owned a beautiful 1770 colonial, the Creary Homestead, in the tiny village of Old Mystic, Connecticut.

A recent and welcome addition expanding the inn is The Historic Haley Tavern, originally a stage coach stop. Restored and beautifully appointed, its rooms include The Ross Haley Chamber with antique furnishings and working fireplace, The Mary Virginia Chamber, a beautiful Early American room with canopy double bed, and The Victorian Nancy Creary Chamber with its own whirlpool tub.

Under Ruth's guardianship, the Red Brook Inn is a colonial showcase. Her collection of furniture and artifacts perfectly complements both the lines and the spirit of the house. All of the rooms are filled with period antiques, from the second-floor bedrooms with their blanket chests, highboys, and early lighting devices, to the first-floor keeping room with its original cooking fireplace, beehive oven, and iron crane and cookware. Each four-poster is coordinated with carefully chosen matching quilts and linens.

A full breakfast, served on the long harvest table in the keeping room, might include quiche, baked or fresh fruit, eggs Benedict, walnut waffles, or berry pancakes.

THE RED BROOK INN, Box 237, Rte. 184 at Wells Rd., Old Mystic, CN 06372; (203) 572-0349; Ruth Keyes and Vern Sasek, hosts. Colonial gem built around 1770. Open year-round. Nine guest rooms; seven with private baths, two with shared baths, six with working fireplaces. Rates: $75–$95 per double room, including a full breakfast. No pets; no smoking in rooms; Visa/MasterCard. Mystic Seaport Museum, Mystic Aquarium, horseback riding, golf, sailing, submarine tour cruises on river, Coast Guard Academy nearby. Excellent dining in area.

DIRECTIONS: take I-95 to exit 89 (Allyn St.); go north 1½ miles to light (Rte. 184 Gold Star Hwy.), Turn right and go east ⅕ mile. Inn is on left.

RIVERWIND

An air of country whimsy

Riverwind is a wonderfully warm bed and breakfast, due largely to Barbara Barlow's enthusiasm. She embodies just the right mix of southern warmth and Yankee forthrightness.

Barbara came to the lower Connecticut River Valley to restore a house on her "vacation" from teaching learning disabled children in Virginia. A comely 1850s house by the green in need of repair caught her attention, and Riverwind fell into her able hands. A year passed while Barbara tore down walls, sanded the old pine floors by hand, painted, and decorated. The inn has come a long way from the days when Barbara dared only bring in a couch, a Coleman stove, and a quilt for herself.

Now, Riverwind communicates an air of country whimsy. It is crisp, spotless, and filled with absorbing details. The engaging décor incorporates modern American crafts and antique accesories and collections. The common rooms resemble a comfortable antiques shop where everything has its place. A decanter of sherry for guests sits on a silver tray, ringed by a half-circle of wooden toy houses that spell WELCOME. Guests settle in as if it were home, especially in the music corner, where Barbara keeps a banjo, guitar, and violin next to the piano.

Pigs are Barbara's favorite motif. Candlelit breakfasts include "piggies," light porcine shaped biscuits to acknowledge the farmers from Barbara's home town of Smithfield, Virginia. The famous southern ham of that city also has its place at the morning buffet, along with fresh fruit and such delectable baked goods as blueberry pound cake and scrumptious coffeecake.

Breakfast room, and a guest room beyond.

RIVERWIND, 209 Main St., Deep River, CT 06417; (203) 526-2014; Barbara Barlow, innkeeper. Open all year. Four guest rooms, all with private baths. Rates: $60 to $70, with full breakfast buffet included. No children; no pets; Visa/MasterCard. Essex steam train, Gillette Castle, Goodspeed Opera House nearby; excellent antiquing and fine restaurants throughout the area.

DIRECTIONS: from I-95, take Rte. 9 north to exit 4. Turn left onto Rte. 9A into Deep River. Riverwind is 1½ miles on the right, just before the town green. From I-91, take Rte. 9 to exit 5. Turn left and continue to Deep River. At the Main St. stop light, turn right onto 9A. Riverwind is on your left just after the town green.

BISHOP'S GATE INN

A theatrical inn near the Goodspeed

Perched on the banks of the Connecticut River, the grand proportions of the Goodspeed Opera House rise in sharp contrast to the surrounding tiny town of East Haddam. The Goodspeed produces musical comedy revivals and one new production a year—including the birth of such hits as *Man of La Mancha, Shenandoah,* and *Annie.* The quality of these productions is such that this house has come to be considered an off-Broadway theater. Besides the Goodspeed, East Haddam is a romantic rural village tailor-made for getting away from it all. Such an escape is easily accomplished by private plane (the airstrip is next to the theater), by boat (the dock is across from the Goodspeed), and, of course, by car.

Bishop's Gate Inn, located in the center of town, is a gem, abetted by the exuberant spirit of owner Julie Bishop and the artful way she has decorated her bed and breakfast inn.

The Jenny Lind Room.

Entering her home, guests immediately come upon the breakfast room. Above the sturdy harvest table hangs a gallery of familiar faces—friends made during Julie's years of working with the Goodspeed actors, many of whom appear on television and in movies. Opposite, a cheering fire crackles in the hearth. Each bedroom is named, and each is decorated with a light hand. For example, the Jenny Lind room is all softness and roses with framed floral prints, rosebud wallpaper, working fireplace, and an antique spool bed draped with a creamy fishnet canopy. The Director's Suite contains part of Julie's stunning marquetry collection, including two oversize twin beds, a chest of drawers, and an arm chair. This suite is made even more dramatic with its beamed cathedral ceiling, private balcony, and "Hollywood" bathroom complete with double sinks, sauna, and sitting area.

BISHOP'S GATE INN, Goodspeed Landing, East Haddam, CT 06423; (203) 873-1677; Julie Bishop, hostess. Colonial built in 1818 and filled with family antiques. Six guest rooms, including one large suite; two with shared baths. Open year-round; closed Mondays. Rates $60–80 single; $75–95 double: $10 additional person. No children under six, no pets; checks accepted. Hearty continental breakfast; picnic lunches can be arranged.

DIRECTIONS: from New York City, Providence, or Boston, take Connecticut Tnpke. (I-95) to exit 69 to Rte. 9. From Rte. 9, take exit 7 to East Haddam. Cross bridge and go straight on Rte. 82 for 1 block. Inn driveway is on left.

Above, one of the exquisite pieces in the marquetry collection sets off some Fred Astaire memorabilia. Left, friends of Julie who have acted at the nearby Goodspeed Opera House.

STONECROFT INN

Refined conviviality

Paul Higgins arrived in East Haddam for a weekend house tour. By the next Monday he had acquired an 1832 clapboard house. "I never once had a second thought," Paul remarked from his place at the firelit breakfast table. Leaving behind twenty-three years as a Boston banker, the inn's dapper host takes immense pleasure from his guests.

The Stonecroft Inn specializes in refined convivialty. One elderly couple celebrated their honeymoon at the inn, and Paul surprised them with a bottle of champagne outside their door. Another time, Paul arranged for a special Sunday brunch for his overnight visitors, most of whom were parents of actors from the nearby Goodspeed Opera House.

A gracious Federal bearing distinguishes each of the five rooms, all of which have private baths.

Buff-gray whites and slate blues evoke a past era, while down comforters modernize the many antiques. Bargello and silk-covered chairs, mahogany dressers, and crystal candelabras help to establish the inn's reputation for genteel comfort.

Guests can talk to Paul as he prepares breakfasts—or "the works" as he calls it. One entrée is featured each day, but this man-of-all-trades is flexible and will take requests. After the meal, guests tend to sit out on the wide side porch and thumb through the before-and-after photo album, one of the inn's first Christmas presents put together by Frank Thomas, whose area photos appear throughout the building.

Five minutes will take you to many of the photographed scenes. In addition, the intriguingly ornate Gillette Castle, the more simple Nathan Hale Schoolhouse, and the steam train in Essex make the Stonecroft Inn an excellent home base for exploring the area.

STONECROFT INN, 17 Main St., East Haddam, CT 06423; (203) 873-1754; Paul Higgins, host. Federal-style clapboard house built as a private residence in 1832. Open year-round. Five guest rooms, all with private baths; some with fireplaces. Rates: $75 to $85. No children under 8; no pets; no credit cards accepted. Canoeing, theatres, and antiquing attract most visitors.

DIRECTIONS: from I-95 take exit 69 to Rte. 9 (exit 7). Follow the signs for the Goodspeed Opera House. The inn is four buildings up from the Goodspeed.

WEST LANE INN

Sample the good life in a private mansion

A New England getaway close to city bustle, the West Lane Inn in historic Ridgefield, Connecticut, is just fifty miles from New York City. This bed and breakfast inn contains more rooms than most, so guests don't always share their morning muffin and coffee with owner Maureen Mayer. But they enjoy the solid comforts evident throughout this grand, early nineteenth-century mansion. Among the amenities generally found only in fine hotels are thick padded carpets and a double thickness of door between adjoining rooms, which helps maintain the prevailing sense of quiet and privacy. Bathrooms are equipped with heated towel racks, full-length mirrors, and, in some cases, bidets. An adjoining house, called the Cottage, contains suites with service kitchens and private decks that open onto a vast expanse of well-manicured lawn. A simple room service menu, an optional full breakfast, king and queen-size beds, a tennis court, and one-day laundry and dry cleaning service make the West Lane Inn a welcome haven for tired wayfarers and business travelers.

WEST LANE INN, 22 West Lane, Ridgefield, CT 06877; (203) 438-7323; Maureen Mayer, hostess. Former private mansion invites guests to sample the good life. Open all year. Fourteen guest rooms in main house, two with working fireplaces; six suites in rear cottage; three suites in ultra-luxurious carriage house; all private baths. Rates: $85 single, $95 double, including continental breakfast; full breakfast available for extra charge. Good dining in area. Children welcome, cribs and playpens available; no pets; major credit cards; no checks. Ridgefield offers Revolutionary War sites, tours, museums; cross-country and downhill skiing.

DIRECTIONS: from NYC, take the FDR to the Major Deegan to Saw Mill Pkwy. Stay on Saw Mill to end and exit onto Rte. 35 going east. Drive approximately 12 miles to Ridgefield. Inn is on Rte. 35.

Left, a cabinet filled with early American glass, pewter, and redware pottery. Above, a portrait of the son of the original owner hangs in the stairway.

BUTTERNUT FARM

An impressive, small museum

Butternut Farm in Glastonbury, Connecticut, is an especially fine example of pre-Revolutionary architecture. The oldest section of the house was built by Jonathan Hale in 1720, a well-to-do gentleman with an eye for fine moldings and a feel for proportion—rare commodities in early homes. By the mid-1700s, a keeping room, "borning room," buttery, and extra bedchambers were added as Hale's family grew.

Present owner Don Reid is a faithful steward to this architectural gem. He loves early American antiques and has collected many excellent examples from the period, including an antique pencil post canopied bed, an exquisite cherry highboy, and pre-Revolutionary bottles and Bennington pottery marbles.

The keeping room has beams bedecked with drying herbs and flowers. An antique settle and variety of chairs surround the large hearth, whose magnitude is completely overshadowed by the second fireplace found in the adjoining dining room. This brick hearth, of mammoth proportions, is teamed up with an oversized antique dining table and bannister-back chairs. An oil painting of Jonathan Hale's son is prominently displayed.

Guest rooms upstairs are decorated with wing-back chairs, wooden chests, and antique hat-boxes. Museum quality, hand-hooked rugs brighten softly gleaming, wide-plank pine floorboards.

Don Reid is a soft-spoken and intellectual man who takes great pride in the home he has created. Continuously occupied since its construction, the house shares its charm with appreciative guests. A carefully tended museum of Americana, this inn is like another world—one that should be visited and revisited to enjoy its many facets.

BUTTERNUT FARM , 1654 Main St., Glastonbury, CT 06033; (203) 633-7197; Don Reid, host. Elegant house built in 1720, with a wealth of interesting architectural detail. Open year-round. Two guest rooms, shared baths; two apartments with private baths. Rates: $45 single, $55 and $65 double. Full breakfast. Checks accepted; no pets; smoking discouraged. Good dining in town and in adjoining Hartford.

DIRECTIONS: take I-84 or I-91 to Rte. 2 exit. Follow Rte. 2 and take exit 8; go right toward Glastonbury Center. Drive to Main St. and turn left. Drive 1.6 miles, and inn is on left.

OLD RIVERTON INN

Two centuries of hospitality

"They're actually out there shoulder to shoulder," says Mark Telford, describing the trout-fishing enthusiasts who fill his inn every year on the third Saturday of April for the Annual Fishing Derby. Just across from the inn, within hearing distance, flows the west branch of the Farmington River. The rushing water makes a sweet lullaby after a long day's drive or a hard day's fishing.

Sleep should come easily in this quaint setting at the end of tiny Riverton's main street. For almost two centuries the inn, originally known as Ives' Tavern, has provided "hospitality for the hungry, thirsty, and sleepy," beginning in 1796 with travelers who came via the Hartford/Albany Turnpike.

As much an inn as a bed and breakfast, Old Riverton hasn't quite caught up with the 1980s; the building was restored in the late 1930s and still reflects the mid part of this century with a casual and unassuming hominess. The atmosphere—more like a grandmother's parlor than a chic new country inn—is simple and comfortable.

The dining room, which is open most of the time (check with the proprietors for more details), houses a collection of old photographs of the inn

Antique clock in the entry hall.

that show the many stages of change and restoration Old Riverton has gone through, including before and after pictures of the porches that had to be torn off to make way for the widening of the street.

Riverton's growth is still relatively minuscule; visitors come mostly for the Hitchcock Chair Factory Store, the John T. Kenney Hitchcock Museum, and the Seth Thomas Factory Outlet, besides the fishing. More active guests can take advantage of the area's sporting activities: whitewater canoeing, tubing, hiking, and horseback riding. There's also downhill and cross-country skiing as well as golf and tennis nearby.

Old Riverton is a charmer—unpretentious, a bit old-fashioned, and everlasting.

OLD RIVERTON INN. Rte. 20, Riverton, CT 06065; (203) 379-8678; Mark and Pauline Telford, innkeepers. Open all year. Twelve guest rooms, all with private baths; one deluxe room with fireplace. Rates: $48 to $76, including full breakfast with table service. Dining at the inn. Children welcome; all major credit cards accepted; some Spanish, French, and Arabic spoken.
DIRECTIONS: from New York City take 95N to 278W, to 684N to 84E, to 8N to Winsted, CT. Take old route 8 to 20E to Riverton. From Boston take the Mass. Pike to I-91 south to Bradley Field, exit 40; then take 20W to Riverton.

The inn faces Farmington River.

Described as Tudor-Bavarian in style.

MANOR HOUSE

One of Connecticut's finest

A beautiful turn-of-the-century mansion, the Manor House in Norfolk, Connecticut, with wood paneled walls and huge stone fireplaces, is the setting for a bed and breakfast inn *par excellence*. Described by some as the most elegant bed and breakfast in Connecticut, the Manor House is the focus of a number of other activities as well.

The innkeepers, who love classical music, have formed a novel partnership with neighbors Carl and Marilee Dudash, who make beautifully decorated harpsichords. The result is the Norfolk Early Music Society and occasional concerts at the Manor House during the winter season, when nearby Tanglewood and Music Mountain are quiescent.

Horse-drawn sleigh and carriage rides are provided for guests during the appropriate season after breakfasts of fresh farm eggs, bacon, orange waffles, blueberry pancakes, french toast, homemade breads, muffins, and coffee.

Diane and Henry Tremblay are new innkeepers who "fell in love at first sight" with the fine old eighteen-room manor. Since there was room enough for both their large family and guests as well, they decided to move in.

The house was built in 1898 by Charles Spofford, designer of London's Underground and son of Ainsworth Rand Spofford, head of the Library of Congress under President Lincoln. The interior is distinctly Victorian, with elegantly carved furniture, ornate fixtures, leaded glass windows, and billowy white curtains.

MANOR HOUSE. P.O. Box 701, Maple Avenue, Norfolk, CT 06058; (203) 542-5690; Diane and Henry Tremblay, hosts. Open all year. Eight guest rooms, most with private baths, some with fireplaces and private balconies. Rates: $50-$70 single, $60-$110 double; includes full breakfast. Children over 12 welcome; no pets (boarding kennels nearby). Yale Summer School of Music and Art an annual event in Norfolk, as well as crafts, antiques, theater, and golf.

DIRECTIONS: take I-84 to exit for Rte. 8 north at Waterbury, Conn. Go north to end of Rte. 8 at Winsted and take Rte. 44 west to Norfolk and Maple Avenue. From Massachusetts take Turnpike west to Rte. 7 exit and go south to Canaan and east on Rte. 44 to Norfolk.

NEW YORK

BAKER'S BED & BREAKFAST

One of the premier bed and breakfasts

This restored stone farmhouse has been used as a Bed and Breakfast ever since it was built in about 1780. Located in an area known as "rest plaus," Dutch for "the rest place," it was a stopover for travelers near a ford in the Roundout River.

Furnished with eighteenth-century country-style antiques and situated on sixteen acres of verdant lawn, it overlooks farms, woods, and mountains. There are herb, rose, and flower gardens and an inviting swimming pool. Guests relax on the first floor of the farmhouse with its colorfully stenciled rooms, its Rumford fireplaces, solarium, and green house with hot tub. Five early American guest rooms, some with private baths, are available year round.

Doug Baker and Linda Delgado, teachers at a local college, are seasoned hosts. Doug, a biologist, loves talking about the local wildlife, restoration, and antiques. Linda, who is fluent in Spanish, is a history buff. Both are gifted cooks, and serve a full gourmet breakfast that includes freshly baked pastries, home grown fruits and vegetables, and their own jams and preserves.

The Shawangunk Mountain Ridge is a magnificent backdrop for the Baker's stone house. Cross-country ski trails and hiking trails abound, and the variety and number of fine restaurants is extraordinary. This area has become a mecca for serious epicures.

BAKER'S BED AND BREAKFAST, RD 2, Box 80, Stone Ridge, NY 12484; (914) 687-9795; Doug Baker and Linda Delgado, hosts. Four rooms with two shared baths and one suite with bath in a 1700s stone house. Open all year. Rates: $58.00 single/double; includes an elegant breakfast of wonderful breads and creative egg specialties served at 9:30 A.M. Two-night minimum required on weekends; overnight guests mid-week only. No children under 12; no pets; no credit cards; checks accepted. Non-smokers preferred but a considerate smoker would be acceptable.

DIRECTIONS: New York State Thruway (I-87) to New Paltz, exit 18. Drive west on Route 299 into New Paltz, turning right onto Rte. 32. Head north for about 6 miles and turn left onto Rte. 213. Proceed through High Falls and turn left onto Rte. 209. Go exactly 1 mile and take the second left off Rte. 209, which is Old Kings Highway; Baker's is midway down the hill on the right.

The 1840 stone cottage.

Left, a breakfast view of the Shawangunk Valley.

THE OLDE POST INN

Live music on weekends

Nestled on the banks of the Hudson River, the town of Cold Spring basks in the beauty of the Palisades across the water. This village is an interesting mix of "local color" and city folk who were lured to the town for its lovely architecture and glorious setting. Among such new residents are Carole Zeller and George Argila. Their home, The Olde Post Inn, sits on a prominent corner of Main Street, two blocks from the river, and is one of the most successful restorations in the village. Built in 1820 as a post office and customs house, the building is on the National Historic Register.

The first floor of this cozy bed and breakfast serves as breakfast room and sitting room. It has open beamwork, hardwood floors, an antique sideboard, comfortable furniture, and a wall of glass that faces the backyard and patio, washing the beautiful woodwork with soft light. Carole collects American crafts, while George, a graduate of the Julliard School of Music, has opened a small cabaret in the basement. In the process of

converting this unused basement space, George and Carole discovered a beehive fireplace, which sets the tone for the tavern. With its own separate entrance, no traffic flows from tavern to inn, except for those guests who spend the evening listening to music. George and other gifted, local musicians play on weekends—and no heavy rock is allowed.

It seems that at least half of Cold Spring is composed of antiques shops and other interesting stores. Besides shopping, visitors can tour the Chapel of Our Lady, an 1834 Greek Revival chapel, which was reproduced in Currier and Ives prints over a century ago, and the elegant eighteenth-century mansion called Boscobel. A short drive away are the Franklin D. Roosevelt National Historic Site and the fifty-room Vanderbilt mansion.

THE OLDE POST INN, 43 Main St., Cold Spring, NY 10516; (914) 265-2510; Carole Zeller and George Argila, hosts. 1820 Federal-style inn was once a post office and customs house. Open all year. Four guest rooms decorated in simple American traditional, shared bath. Rates $45 to $60 per room, including continental breakfast with homemade breads. Excellent dining nearby. Older children welcome; no pets; Visa/MasterCard. Tavern downstairs features live music on weekend nights.

DIRECTIONS: from west side of Hudson take Palisades Pkwy. to Bear Mt. Bridge. Turn left on Rte. 9D and proceed into Cold Spring. Turn left at light onto Main St. From NYC, take Taconic Pkwy. to Rte. 301, Cold Spring exit. Also from NYC, take Rte. 9 to Rte. 301, which becomes Main St. at Cold Spring.

Left, the view from the breakfast room into the living room.

CAPTAIN SCHOONMAKER'S

Gastronomical breakfasts

The 1760 stone house on the Kriegs' property is the main house, but is only one of three accommodating structures that comprise Captain Schoonmaker's. Just beyond the driveway sits a whimsically restored barn, where the most asked-after rooms look out over the brook. The other most often-requested rooms are hidden away down the street in the old canal lock-tender's quarters. Guests have to walk the half mile from the canal-side cottage to the main house, but it's a welcome activity after Julia Krieg's amazingly ample breakfast.

Talkative and perky, hostess Julia won't take no for an answer. Her guests groan with surfeited delight by the fourth course at breakfast. Saturday's usual menu begins with broiled grapefruit and moves on to an herb-cheese soufflé accompanied by sausage almost candied with New York maple syrup. The meal continues with a halo of apricot and honey danish. Is breakfast over? No; with theatrical timing, Julia again appears: this time with cherry strudel. Hence, the groan.

CAPTAIN SCHOONMAKER'S 1760 STONE HOUSE, Box 37, Route 237, High Falls, NY 12440; (914) 687-7946; Sam and Julia Krieg, hosts. Open year-round. Three guests rooms in the main stone house, four rooms in the carriage house/barn, four rooms in the Towpath House. Two rooms with fireplace; shared baths. Rates: $60 to $70. Full breakfast. Children welcome during the week, over 6 only, on weekends; no pets; no credit cards. Hiking, boating, tubing, swimming, scuba diving (lake), horseback riding, golf, wineries, and summer theater nearby.

DIRECTIONS: from Kingston take Rte. 209W to Ellenville to 213E to Rosendale (left turn), about 3 miles to the house, which is on the right. Sam will pick guests up at the bus station in Rosendale.

MAPLE SHADE BED & BREAKFAST

A country oasis

Hidden away in some of New York's most beautiful countryside, Cooperstown sits on the shores of scenic Lake Otsego. There's nothing pretentious about this sophisticated back-country oasis. The small shopping district is well-organized to fend off insensitive developers, and so Main Street flourishes as it did years ago with stores and a 1920s movie theatre. Even the National Baseball Hall of Fame hasn't intruded on the town's quiet sense of pride and practicality.

Judge William Cooper settled here in 1786 and built the village's first two log structures. His son, James Fenimore, immortalized the area in his books.

The tone is casual and friendly. White and pastel colors define the American country theme, and set off the slate blue carpeting. Old oak, new brass, and wicker blend together into a pleasing package presided over by congenial hosts Robert and Linda Crampton, natives of the area.

MAPLE SHADE BED AND BREAKFST, R.D. #1, Box 105A, Milford, NY 13807; (607) 547-9530; Robert and Linda Crampton, hosts. Open all year. Three guest rooms share two baths; one suite has private bath. Rates: $48; children, $5 additional; includes hearty breakfast. No pets; no smoking; Visa/MasterCard. Good restaurants are abundant.

DIRECTIONS: from the south, take the New York State Thruway to exit 21 (Catskill) to Rte. 145 north. Turn onto Rte. 20 west, then Rte. 28 south through Cooperstown. The inn is four miles from town, on the right. From I-88, take Rte. 28 north. The inn is on the left.

J. P. SILL HOUSE

A showcase of wallpapers

Formal elegance betrays a studied warmth in the J.P. Sill House, a showcase of impeccably designed and printed wallpapers. The handscreened "room sets" may include as many as seven different yet harmonious patterns. All are based on original works by turn-of-the-century artists. Innkeeper Joyce Bohlman discovered the California firm of Bradbury & Bradbury from a newspaper article; an inquiry and a visit to the firm convinced her to paper the house with these carefully chosen designs. Hiring a paperhanger was no problem, either; one of Joyce's brothers is a professional. The results are spectacular.

The green-hued formal dining room carries an Eastlake frieze paper initially reproduced for the Cameron-Stanford House in Oakland, California; the fill paper, a graceful willow pattern, is attributed to William Morris. Both become richer when sunlight filters in through the room's French doors that open onto one of the inn's porches.

Joyce kept pieces of the wallpapers with her for six months wherever she traveled, buying

material and accessories to fit the beautifully appointed rooms, all of which are furnished with antiques to match the ambiance of the papers: an Eastlake bed stands at counterpoint to the green marble fireplace in the Master Bedroom; a brass and white-iron bed complements the soft peach and blue of the Shell Room. Linens and lace add to the details.

The house seduces its guests. A long tin bathtub invites visitors to take a luxurious break—bath powder already provided. Seasonal fruit baskets or homemade sweets adorn the rooms as appropriately as the objets d'arts, and potpourri scents the air.

Expect the same quality of attention at breakfast. Simply prepared gourmet fare comes presented on china. White linen napkins and silver service complete this unabashed indulgence.

THE J.P. SILL HOUSE, 63 Chestnut St., Cooperstown, NY 13326; (607) 547-2633; Joyce Bohlman, innkeeper. Open all year. 1894 Italiante Victorian on state and national historic registers. Five guest rooms share two baths. Rates: $55 to $65, slightly higher on Hall of Fame Weekend. Two-night minimum for summer weekends; four-night minimum for Hall of Fame Weekend. Full, elegant breakfast. No pets, kennel nearby; no children under 13; no smoking. Year-round sports activities: Lake Otsego; Baseball Hall of Fame; Farmer's Museum; Fenimore House; antiquing, auctions, summer theatre, and opera.

DIRECTIONS: once in Cooperstown, ask inn for location of the house.

More Bradbury and Bradbury wallpaper, in the Downstairs Parlor, left, and in the Peacock Room, above.

STAGECOACH INN

Its own brand of romance

Bustling Lake Placid Village lies tucked between two shimmering bodies of water. Shallow and tranquil Mirror Lake laps up to the town's center. Just a few miles north, Lake Placid serves as the village's reservoir, reaching spring-fed depths of over 300 feet—an angler's paradise with native fish as well as upwards of 10,000 rainbow and lake trout stocked by the state each year.

Sports activities are a large part of village life. Many of the 1980 Winter Olympic structures continue to bring in world-class championships throughout the year.

The 1833 clapboard Stagecoach Inn sits two miles northwest of the ski jumps on a back street away from traffic and village noise. Rustic and casual, the inn delivers its own brand of romance to its guests. Warmed by a fireplace, the two-story cathedral-ceilinged living room invites sitting back and enjoying the Adirondack-style details that once marked an era of extravagant parties and stimulating conversation. Yellow birch logs and twigs form the mantel, bookshelves, and support beams, as well as an imposing banister that leads to a second floor balcony.

The view down to the living room makes a still life *extraordinaire*. A deer head rests comfortably above the fireplace, a working Mason and Hamlin organ stands to the left, and on the side wall crossed snowshoes hang over framed photos of former innkeepers Mr. and Mrs. Lyons.

The other common area, the dining room, encloses its visitors with Georgia pine on the walls, ceiling, and floors. A cozy fire reflects in the wood's sheen, casting an amber radiance on the morning meal—a perfect touch to start any day.

THE STAGECOACH INN, Old Military Road, Lake Placid, NY 12946; (518) 523-9474; Peter Moreau, inn owner; Lin Witte, innkeeper. Open all year. Six cozy guest rooms, two with private baths, one with fireplace. Rates: $30 to $35, single; $45 to $65, double: $5 for an additional person. Children welcome; inquire about pets. Sports activities nearby include golf, hiking, rock climbing, trout fishing, horseback riding. Skating school ice shows every Saturday night in session; Mercedes Circuit horse show in summer.

DIRECTIONS: from the Adirondack Northway (Rte. 87), take Rte. 73N for 30 miles. Bear left just past the ski jumps (where the Saranac Lake sign is pointing). The inn is about two miles down on the left.

THE ROSE MANSION AND GARDENS

Rochester's hidden treasure

The inn, Rochester's hidden treasure, stands behind a towering stone wall, and includes an impressive garden designed by George Ellwanger, a prominent nurseryman who owned the house.

Ellwanger planted the grounds with the idea that the gardens would serve as a continuation of the house—as an outdoor room. The gravel paths offer a rich variety, from boxwood hedge borders to a lavender walk with a weeping cherry tree, copper beech trees, and old pear trees. In all, more than seventy-five kinds of flowering and green plants are represented, including some beds of rare unusual roses.

The formal but welcoming house is as grand as its gardens. At the landing midway between the first and second floors is an 1887 Hook and Hastings pipe organ tucked into the wall; the pipes rise monumentally up to the high ceiling. The organ inspired Stephen and Jeanne Ferranti to organize a Christmas spectacular. The event, which takes place in even-numbered years, has featured the German Youth Orchestra and highlighted a nineteen-foot tree in the great hall landing, with children forming a line up the stairs, each one holding a candle.

Most of the year, however, a refined quiet reigns in the house. A Chickering grand piano and a chess set provide an evening's entertainment in the Victorian Great Room, which still displays a silk-and-cotton blend beige tapestry wallpaper, a detail lost in most renovations. French doors open onto the porch that fronts the garden, and another pair leads into the dining room where an elegant continental breakfast is served.

Each of the ten spacious guest rooms is named for a rose, and all are comfortably and aristocratically furnished with antiques.

THE ROSE MANSION AND GARDENS, 625 Mt. Hope Ave., Rochester, NY 14620; (716) 546-5426; Stephen and Jeanne Ferranti, innkeepers. Open all year. Some French and Spanish spoken. Ten guest rooms, three with fireplaces; suite arrangements available. All with private baths. Rates: $65 to $90, single; $70 to $95, double; additional person, $10. Continental breakfast included. Children over 11 welcome; no pets; smoking in the guest rooms only. American Express/MasterCard/Visa.

DIRECTIONS: from east and Thruway exit 45, take Rte. 490 west. Follow sign for Rte. 390 north, Airport. Bear left. Take exit 16 (Rte. 15 and 15A). From exit proceed straight, follow sign for Rte. 15 north. Turn right onto Rte. 15. Pass Elmwood Ave; continue about 1 mile. Rose Mansion and Gardens is on the left. From the south and Thruway exit 46, take Rte. 390 north to exit 16. Follow directions above.

Swarthmore, and Camelot sitting room beyond—the names of roses.

The house is colorful, gay, and fanciful.

UJJALA'S BED & BREAKFAST

A bit of California in upstate New York

Ujjala's Bed and Breakfast vibrates with a California sensibility. Her charming Victorian frame cottage sits amidst a grove of apple, pear, and quince trees, and is painted in luscious hues of lilac, periwinkle, and plum. Ujjala renovated her home and added skylights, contemporary stained glass, lots of plants, whimsical ceramics, and flowers.

The focus at Ujjala's is on health. With a background in "body therapy"—Shiatsu and deep-relaxation therapy—she has given courses in stress management to university students and corporate business people, and she was filmed for the television special "The Body Human." Ujjala is also an able cook who specializes in "vegetarian gourmet" cuisine. Her full breakfast includes homemade whole grain breads, fresh fruits, and eggs, and she goes out of her way to accommodate people on special diets. If you've always wanted to cleanse your system with a fast or a special diet, a stay at Ujjala's may be in order. Link a well-balanced and healthful diet with Ujjala's therapy and you can come away from this bed and breakfast feeling like a brand new person.

UJJALA'S BED AND BREAKFAST, 2 Forest Glen Rd., New Paltz, NY 12561; (914) 255-6360; Ujjala Schwartz, hostess. Open all year. Four guest rooms and one warm-weather studio, shared bath. Rates $50 to $60 double, including full breakfast. Afternoon tea and coffee, sherry in winter. Excellent dining nearby. No children; no pets; smoking discouraged; no credit cards. Inn offers exercise and relaxation therapy programs.

DIRECTIONS: from N.Y. State Thruway, take New Paltz Exit 18. Go left on Rte. 299 into town and turn left at light onto Rte. 208 S. Drive 3½ miles, passing Dressel Farm on right, take second right onto Forest Glen Rd. Ujjala's is driveway on left.

THE GOLDEN EAGLE INN

An idyllic spot on the mighty Hudson

The location of The Golden Eagle is idyllic; the yard sweeps gently to the edge of the mighty Hudson. This stretch of the river is especially arresting, for across the way, built on a towering granite cliff, sits West Point Military Academy in grey gothic grandeur.

The inn is a lovely, soft red brick, three-story building. Embellished with a broad veranda, it feels like a transplant from a warmer climate. Inside, the rooms are decorated with an eye to incorporating bright and pleasing color. The focal point of one large suite is a half-canopied bed strewn with white calla lilies on a peach background. Upstairs, rooms vary from spring bouquet colors of yellow, green, and pink to a lucious blend of blues, purples, and rose. George and Stephanie Templeton spent years in the design trade, and their light, professional touch works well. George is also an accomplished watercolorist, whose paintings brighten the walls of the parlor, breakfast room (used only when the weather prohibits dining on the veranda), and many of the bedrooms. Besides the continental breakfast of fresh fruit, croissants, and tea or coffee, the Templetons offer luncheon on the veranda during the warm months of the year. The menu might include overstuffed "riverboat" sandwiches, quiche, fresh fruit plates, soup, "the best chocolate cake in the world," and George's secret recipe, a drink known as "fresh fruit café."

The minute town of Garrison is dominated by the train station. Visitors from New York City need not bring a car. They can simply catch a train from Grand Central Station, which drops them off close to the inn's front door. Trains are available to take diners into Cold Spring in the evening and return them to the comforts of the inn afterwards.

Left, the Golden Eagle, to which you can travel by train, seaplane, or auto. Above, much attention has been lavished on the guest rooms.

THE GOLDEN EAGLE INN, Garrison's Landing, NY 10524; (914) 424-3067; George and Stephanie Templeton, hosts. Federal-style building, built in 1848 as hotel for visitors to West Point. Open most of year; closed for spring vacations. Six guest rooms, one a suite with private, handicap-accessible entrance. Private baths. Rates by room: $65–75; $15 for third person ($10 during week). Reservations mandatory; advance reservation with check only. Children discouraged and not accepted on weekends; no pets. Continental breakfast. Variety of restaurants within 15-minute drive. Museums, hiking. canoeing, vineyards, West Point nearby.

DIRECTIONS: from south, take Palisades Pkwy. to Bear Mountain Bridge. Cross bridge and take Rte. 9D to junction of Rte. 403. Turn left onto Rte. PC-12 toward river. Follow road to stop sign. Turn left over small bridge and turn left. Inn is 75 feet on right. From Cold Spring, take Rte. 9D to junction of Rte. 403. Turn right (PC-12) and follow directions above. Note: Inn can be reached by train from Grand Central Station, by boat on the Hudson, or by seaplane, with mooring at adjacent Highland Yacht Club.

PENNSYLVANIA

FAIRWAY FARM

Added attraction: the only trumpet museum in the world

Fairway Farm's claim to fame is its proximity to "the one and only trumpet museum in the world," says Franz Streitwieser, the world-renowned brass musician and historian who founded the museum and opened his house to visitors. Since his children have left home for school, Franz and his wife Katherine have tried to create a European-style bed and breakfast in the tradition of southern Germany and Austria.

The most striking antiques in the household are the Bavarian hand-painted blanket chests dating from 1805 and 1846. A blue-hued bed made in the Black Forest, with a heart-and-floral motif is a bit younger but just as beautiful.

The atmosphere is casual and nonchalant. featuring a wood sauna, spring-fed swimming pool, and asphalt tennis court. Guests are free to roam down to the gazebo or to the pond.

The real fun here, though, is next door. For a suggested donation of $2.50, Franz will take you on a personal tour of the museum, sometimes even unlocking a case to give a musical demonstration. Over four hundred brass instruments fill the cathedral-ceilinged building, including hunting horns, echo instruments, and the world's smallest trumpet. The museum opens up for chamber concerts and lectures, and a musical event is usually scheduled in the gazebo in midsummer.

Franz and Katherine will also guide visitors to the area's many activities. Ski areas are only forty-five minutes away; the Poconos, one hour. The countryside is rife with antique shops. You might say that a stay at Fairway Farm is a well-orchestrated, harmonious getaway!

FAIRWAY FARM BED AND BREAKFAST, Fairway Farm, Vaughn Rd., Pottstown, PA 19464; (215) 326-1315; Katherine and Franz Streitwieser, hosts. German and French spoken. Open September through July. Four guest rooms plus adjoining hallway with Dutch-style foot-to-foot twin beds. Private baths in all except hallway room. Rates: $35, single; $50, double; includes a hearty breakfast with farm-smoked bacon and fresh eggs. Children welcome; no pets; smoking in the den only; no credit cards.

DIRECTIONS: from the Pennsylvania Turnpike, take exit 23 to Rte. 100 north. Turn right onto Rte. 724 and again onto Vaughan Rd. Follow the signs from there.

Left, a stunning display of trumpets in the museum.

Tiffany windows depict the sea at morning, noon, and night.

HARRY·PACKER MANSION

A spectacular wedding present

The age of elegance produced some of the most spectacular architecture of all time. The Harry Packer Mansion is no exception. "An architect used this house as his inspiration for the Haunted Mansion in Walt Disney World," remarked Patricia Handwerk, who, with her husband Bob, is painstakingly restoring the house, keeping the old ceiling paintings, gilt cove work, and other particulars intact wherever possible.

Many of the elaborate, ornate extravagances that characterize the house can be attributed to Asa Packer, the founder of the Lehigh Valley Railroad, who presented the mansion to his son as a wedding present in 1874. From the very outside the noble details begin. Minton tile paves the floor of the Corinthian-columned veranda. The main entrance's 450-pound, etched-glass paneled doors open onto oak parquet floors. The Reception Room, the only common area not furnished according to Packer's plan, sports a walnut mantel and red pine floors. The adjoining library boasts an intricately sculpted mantel of sixteenth-century Caen stone that came from a British manor house. Above the fireplace rests a handsome niche of rich mahogany that follows through into dark paneled walls and a solid-beamed ceiling with oak inserts. The bathroom off the library retains the original mahogany toilet seat, a delicate Limoges basin set in a pink marble sink highlighted by silver spigots. The effect is entrancing.

Opposite the grand double parlors, though, is the house's most eloquent room. Three Tiffany windows from 1881 depict morning, noon, and

night by the seashore, casting multicolored rays onto the Chippendale dining set and the unusual wood carpet, a pattern of inlaid woods—mahogany, cherry. oak, ebony, and chestnut—designed to resemble a rug with a central pattern, border, corner fans, and even a floor mat by the entry.

The bedrooms, slightly less formidable, are no less formal. Guest curl up to sleep in style.

THE HARRY PACKER MANSION, Packer Hill, Jim Thorpe, PA 18229; (717) 325-8566. Some French spoken. Open year round. Second Empire stone-and-brick mansion with cast iron trim. Eight spacious guest rooms, four with private bath. Rates: $50; suite, $100; includes a full, elegant breakfast in the dining room. Coffee or breakfast in bed on request. Children are welcome; no pets; smoking in common rooms only. American Express/MasterCard/Visa. Steam train and Victorian high tea on summer weekends, carriage rides on Sundays in warm weather; mule and horseback riding; whitewater canoeing; Lake Mauch Chunk nearby. Call for details concerning Mystery Weekends, balls, and other special events.

DIRECTIONS: from the Pennsylvania Turnpike Northeast Extension, take exit 34. Continue 6 miles south on Rte. 209. Follow signs up the hill to the mansion.

The ladies' Parlor.

The Suite, with fabric covered walls reproducing the original.

Ray Constance Hearne making breakfast.

SPRING HOUSE

"Back to basics"

Ray Constance Hearne, a gracious and wise hostess, restored this 1798 family home with a deliberateness guided by a preservationist's philosophy: "Buildings should show their age and reflect their history". Guests wandering through her house see remnant patches of old wall treatments peeking through the whitewash, or, up-

stairs, the stenciling that dates back to the 1820s.

When Ray mentions "back to basics," she means antiques, feather beds, down puffs, flannel sheets, and wholesome foods. "I get eggs from chickens that run around outside and eat grass." The tangle of blue and red ribbons that hang by her kitchen window attest to her skills as baker, wine maker, and cook.

The Spring House is a balm for tiredness or frazzled nerves. A weekend here matched with a trip to the nearby Allegro Vineyards, the Susquehanna River, and one of the locale's fine restaurants combines for an excellent cure.

SPRING HOUSE, Muddy Creek Forks, York County, Airville, PA 17302; (717) 927-6906; Ray Constance Hearne, innkeeper. Open year round. Spanish and French spoken. Five guest rooms, two with private baths. Rates: $50 to $80, including a hearty breakfast. Refreshment served on arrival. Children welcome; pets boarded nearby (reservations recommended); no smoking; no credit cards.

DIRECTIONS: from the east take Rte. 202 to the Pennsylvania Turnpike. Pick up Rte. 202 again at King of Prussia (exit Rte. 30 west) and take the Rte. 30 bypass. Go south on 41 to Atglen, 372 west across the Susquehanna, and a right onto 74 north. At Brogue, turn left at the post office. Muddy Creek Forks is 5 miles; at the bottom of the hill is Spring House.

A fascinating collection of paintings decorate the walls.

Above, handmade beds and quilts in the guest rooms. Right, the first-floor breakfast room.

SMITHTON

Pennsylvania Dutch hospitality

In the mid-1700s Henry and Susana Miller were devout members of the Ephrata Community, a Protestant monastic religious group founded by charismatic leader Johann Conrad Beissel. As "outdoor members," the Millers lived by a more relaxed discipline than the majority of disciples, who were celibate and ascetic. The Millers' home, a sturdy stone structure that served as a tavern and stagecoach stop, sat on a hill overlooking the Community Cloister. The Cloister was a remarkably beautiful group of medieval German buildings constructed along the banks of the Cocalico Creek, where Beissel and his followers lived and worked. Although the community of believers declined over the years, the Cloister remains—as does the Millers' home, which is now an inn called Smithton.

Smithton is a warm and welcoming home, and Dorothy Graybill, a Lancaster County native, is the gracious hostess. In this inn guests are steeped in two centuries of history while treated to the the true spirit of Pennsylvania Dutch hospitality. Throughout the house, from the airy kitchen and adjoining dining room to the deluxe, two-story suite complete with Jacuzzi bath, they will enjoy the special attention that is given to wood, from handmade beds and Windsor chairs to hand-fashioned latches and hinges, their design taken from a Cloister pattern. The focal point of each bedroom is the traditional bright and cheerful, handstitched quilt—made by one of the local Mennonite ladies, of course. Extra-large, square down pillows, perfect props for a good read in bed, and soft flannel nightshirts hanging behind each door are just two of many thoughtful and creative touches. Each morning a full breakfast is served by Dorothy, who is assisted by a "plain person," local parlance for the Mennonite and Amish people.

SMITHTON, 900 W. Main St., Ephrata, PA 17522; (717) 733-6094; Dorothy Graybill, hostess. Pennsylvania Dutch spoken. Rustic stone house built in 1762. Five guest rooms plus one suite, all with private baths. Open year-round. Rates: $35 to $75 rooms, $105 suite, $10 third person (no fee for infants). Continental breakfast. Interesting choice of restaurants in area. Children and pets accepted; checks accepted; must prepay in full.

DIRECTIONS: from north or south, take Rte. 222 to the Ephrata exit. Turn west on Rte. 322 (Ephrata's Main Street) and drive 2½ miles to Smithton.

MAPLE LANE

In the heart of Amish country

It's Marion Rohrer's touch that makes Maple Lane so special; she adds a homespun air to an otherwise modern colonial home. Pierced parchment lampshades glow into the evenings, when guests curl up in one of Marion's or her daughter-in-law's quilts. Similar coverlets are offered for sale in a nook on the first floor. If the Rohrer family offerings don't fit the bill, Marion kindly directs serious buyers to neighboring Amish farms.

Longtime residents of Paradise, the Rohrers own and operate a working dairy farm with about two hundred head of cows. Ed welcomes guests to watch the milking, and he invites children to help feed the calves. Guests and grandchildren are the Rohrer's hobbies, so Ed loves to answer questions about the farm while Marion keeps track of all the auctions, farmers' markets, and antiques shops.

This is the heart of Amish country. Although Maple Lane is not an Amish farm—three of its neighbors are—the Rohrers maintain a refreshing air of simplicity and kindness.

MAPLE LANE GUEST HOUSE, 505 Paradise Lane, Paradise, PA 17562; (717) 687-7479. Ed and Marion Rohrer, hosts. Open year-round. Four guests rooms with two baths. Modern two-story colonial within sight of a 1785 stone house and Amish farms. Rates: $30. Includes continental breakfast. Children welcome; no pets; smokers encouraged to use the outside porch in warm weather. Two-night minimum on weekends from April through October. Tourist attractions, shopping, antiquing, historic homes nearby. Pennsylvania Dutch restaurants in abundance.

DIRECTIONS: turn south on Rte. 896 from Rte. 30. Proceed to Strasbourg; turn left on Rte. 896 at the traffic light and continue 1½ miles out of town. Turn right at the sign for the Timberline Lodge. Maple Lane is the first farm on the left.

Cross stitch sampler made by the hostess.

Creative American fare

If a home with two rooms to let is one end of the bed and breakfast scale, then the Duling-Kurtz House & Country Inn represents the other end. Unlike most inns, this pleasant, clean renovated barn provides such amenities as a telephone and videodisc player in every guest room as well as a heat lamp in a modern bathroom.

The appointments are crisp-looking contemporary reproductions that fit the time and reflect the style of the person for whom each room is named. The light and airy Dolly Madison room with a basket-and-floral paper highlights a white

wicker ensemble. The more sedate Betsy Ross, a room of deep maroon, features primitive country and rattan furniture. The blue-gray and gray color scheme of the James Buchanan room helps to establish a Federal feeling. There are fifteen guest rooms in all, including three suites with sitting area and convertible sofa.

The inn connects via a covered, pillared walkway to a 150 year old stone house with a graceful white enclosed porch on the first floor and open-air veranda on the second. Reserve in advance to eat in one of the seven intimate dining rooms that comprised the original house. Co-owner George Stadler, a graduate of the Culinary Institute of America, prepares fine, creative American fare. For special events ask for the *ne plus ultra* Duling-Kurtz Room, which seats two or four in a windowed nook set off from the rest of the dining area with curtains. The $25 rental fee includes a memento of the occasion: silver napkin rings engraved with the celebration's date.

Continental breakfast on a silver tray with the daily paper arrives at your door at a preappointed hour. Freshly squeezed orange juice, croissants, and freshly baked muffins are house specialties.

The inn benefits from its central location—within an hour from Longwood Gardens and Winterthur to the south, Valley Forge National Park to the northeast, and Lancaster County to the west.

DULING-KURTZ HOUSE & COUNTRY INN, South Whitford Rd., Exton, PA 19341; (215) 524-1830; Ken Sellers and George Stadler, proprietors. Italian, German, and Arabic spoken. Open all year. Fifteen guest rooms, all with private baths; suites available. Rates: $75 to $120; each additional person, $15; includes continental breakfast in bed. Children welcome; call ahead if traveling with a pet; all major credit cards accepted. Excellent dining in area. Indoor/outdoor tennis, golf, and regional attractions.

DIRECTIONS: from Route 30 east continue on through the intersection of Rtes. 100 and 30. The turnoff for the inn is ¼ mile west of the junction. Look for the sign.

Guest rooms, left, are fresh and cheerful, and the main living room, above, is calm and elegant.

BARLEY SHEAF FARM

Romance and charm for blithe spirits

A sense that all's right with the world is the hallmark of the best inns. Barley Sheaf Farm in Bucks County emanates that wonderful feeling of security and comfort.

The property has attracted blithe and sophisticated spirits throughout its life, most notably when it was owned by playwright George S. Kaufman, and weekend guests included Moss Hart, Lillian Hellman, S.J. Perlman, and Alexander Woollcott.

Today, Ann and Don Mills' guests may stay in the farmhouse or in one of three bedrooms in the converted ice house. Bedrooms in the main house vary in size, but total charm is assured in each. A two-room suite furnished with an impressive brass sleigh bed, broad and comfortable upholstered couch, working fireplace, and French doors with handpainted privacy screen is the largest bedchamber. The separate ice house, comprising a living room with three very individual, country-style bedrooms, is tailor-made for couples traveling together.

A great percentage of the foodstuffs for a truly splendid breakfast come from the farm; the Millses raise chickens, keep bees, and harvest a large crop of raspberries each year. A puffy soufflé made from fresh eggs, buttery biscuits dripping with Barley Sheaf honey, feather-light pancakes and fresh raspberry sauce garnished with nutmeg-flecked sour cream, a homemade sausage ring, apple crêpes filled with cheese, nuts, and raisins and napped with homemade apple syrup, a sour cream coffee cake—need one say more to describe total satisfaction?

BARLEY SHEAF FARM, Box 10, Rte. 202, Holicong, PA 18928; (215) 794-5104; Ann and Don Mills, and Don Mills, Jr., hosts. French spoken by Ann. Open February 14 through last weekend before Christmas; weekends only January to February 14. Six guest rooms in main house, plus three in cottage; private baths. Rates: $80 to $120, $15 per extra person. Full breakfast served. Wide selection of restaurants in area. No children under eight; no pets; checks accepted.

DIRECTIONS: from Philadelphia, take I-95 north to exit 332 (Newtown). Turn left at exit and drive to third light, turning right onto Rte. 532. Take first left at Goodnoes Restaurant and then turn right onto Rte. 413 north. Follow 413 for about twelve minutes and turn right at intersection of Rte. 202. Farm is on the right about a five-minute drive on 202.

THE INN AT FORDHOOK FARM

Burpee seeds branches out

The Inn at Fordhook Farm stands as a monument to quiet, old world elegance. Three generations of the Burpee family, purveyors of world-class seeds, entertained guests in this charming, predominantly eighteenth-century fieldstone residence. The tradition is continuing since Blanche Burpee Dohan and Jonathan Burpee, the firm's founder's grandchildren, opened the house as an eminently comfortable bed and breakfast.

Each of the five rooms, named for different family members, has its own appeal, although honeymoon couples tend to gravitate to the spacious Burpee Room with its colonial revival fireplace and private balcony or to the stately Atlee Room, accented with leaded glass windows, fireplace, and balcony. The smaller Curtiss Room is a cozy nook with slanted roof and gorgeous view of the grounds. Double pocket doors distin-

guish the Torrance Room, as sunshine, peach hues, and three mirrored closet panels enhance the Simmons Room. The linden tree outside is a "a favorite haunt of the hoot owl," says Blanche.

Trees form an outstanding backdrop here along with the numerous gardens, including former seed-trial beds. Daffodils carpet the lawn's edge in spring, while marigolds last until the first frost. Lilacs, wisteria, and perennials dot the grounds amid gingkos, sycamores, dogwood, magnolia, rhododendrons and azalea, all befitting the gracious home of one of the most famous men in seed history.

THE INN AT FORDHOOK FARM, 105 New Britain Rd., Doylestown, PA 18901; (215) 345-1766; Blanche Burpee Dohan and Laurel Raymond, innkeepers. Open all year. French and German spoken. Five guest rooms, 3 with private baths, 2 with fireplaces; suite arrangement available. Rates: $60 to $90; additional person, $17. Full farm breakfast included; afternoon tea served on the terrace. Children over 12 welcome; no pets; smoking on the terrace only; Visa/MasterCard. Tubing, canoeing, rafting, swimming, tennis, horseback riding, ice skating, cross-country skiing; Mercer Museum and Moravian Tile Works; antiquing. Excellent dining in the area.

DIRECTIONS: The Inn at Fordhook Farm is located at Rte. 202 and the 611 bypass, 1.6 miles west of Doylestown. From Doylestown follow Rte. 202 south past the hospital and over the 611 bypass. Turn left on New Britain Rd. (first road on your left next to Delaware Valley College). The entrance to Fordhook is ¼ mile on your left through two stone pillars. Follow the drive over the little bridge to the large stone house on the right.

Bottom left, the Simmons Room, named after a relative. Overleaf, the grand house and sweeping lawns.

PINEAPPLE HILL

The symbol of hospitality

The streets of New Hope are thickly lined with chic shops and restaurants that cater to the great flow of tourists visiting Bucks County each year. This bustling village is the county's hub. Just four miles from New Hope's commercial center, Pineapple Hill offers the intimacy and comfort of a family home with the convenience of the town's close proximity.

In colonial times, the pineapple symbolized hospitality. True to its name, Pineapple Hill offers travelers comfort and friendly intimacy in an authentic colonial setting.

The hosts, Randy and Suzie Leslie, have decorated their home with American country furnishings, mostly from Pennsylvania and Virginia: antique quilts, coverlets and crocks, folk and primitive art. Suzie's superb collection of antique spools is displayed throughout the house.

The house was built in several sections, and five antique-filled guest rooms are thus divided, three in two second-floor wings and two under the third-floor eaves. Two separate suites are perfect for families or for two couples.

One of the most striking features of Pineapple Hill is its backyard stone ruins. Where a colonial barn once stood, there is a swimming pool made private and scenic by the barn's preserved foundations.

The grounds are ideal for walking, jogging, and, in winter, cross-country skiing. The Delaware Canal towpath borders the grounds and invites canoers and rafters.

PINEAPPLE HILL, 1324 River Road, New Hope, PA 18938; (215) 862-9608; Randy and Suzie Leslie, hosts. Open year-round. Five guest rooms including two suites, three with private baths. Rates: $45-$85, including generous continental breakfast. Snacks and beverages always available. Children during week; no pets; no smoking; American Express, checks accepted. Swimming pool on premises, excellent dining in area.

DIRECTIONS: from Philadelphia, take I-95 to New Hope/Yardley exit. Drive north on Taylorsville Rd. to junction with Rte. 32. Inn is 100 yards north on 32, second driveway on right. From New York City, take New Jersey Tpke. south to exit 10. Take I-287 north to Rte. 22 and 22 west to Rte. 202. Take 202 south to New Hope exit (first in Penn.). Drive south through New Hope on River Rd. (Rte. 32). Continue 4.6 miles beyond traffic light. Inn is on left across from Thorpe Farm sign.

A most elegant setting for breakfast.

BACKSTREET INN

The best breakfast in town

BackStreet Inn is the unique creation of innkeepers Rolf Braun and Nicolas Laurino. The Inn, built in 1750, is nestled in three acres complete with its own swimming pool and wishing well. Historic New Hope is a short drive away.

Upon arrival guests will discover a lace-covered basket filled with chocolate chip cookies in their room. Special occasions such as birthdays and anniversaries are remembered with a celebratory bottle of champagne or bouquet of balloons.

The Inn features, among other amenities, the best breakfast in town. Breakfast, served in a sun-filled dining room and on impeccable china, begins with fresh fruit, juice, and homemade muffins. Specialities of the inn include French toast smothered in liqueur and strawberry sauce.

But the real specialty of the inn is its innkeepers. Rolf and Nick are ideal hosts: courteous, thoughtful, and extremely enthusiastic and entertaining. Guests are photographed for Rolf and Nick's album and invited to comment on their stay at the inn in a guest book. The most telling review of an inn is, of course, that of its guests. Judging from the guest book, the review of the BackStreet Inn is a unanimous "rave".

BACKSTREET INN, 144 Old York Road, New Hope, PA 18938; (215) 862-9571; Rolf Braun and Nicolas Laurino, hosts. Some German spoken. Open year-round. Seven guest rooms, including one suite. Two rooms with private baths, others share. Rates: From $69 to $110 including full breakfast and tax. No children; no pets; smoking permitted; MasterCard/Visa/American Express. Swimming pool on premises, croquet on lawn, 3½ acres of park-like grounds.

DIRECTIONS: from Philadelphia, take I-95 to New Hope/Yardley exit. Go left to Route 32 (River Road) and take a left to traffic light in center of New Hope. Make another left and proceed to MacDonald's, and then make another left for one block, and then a right to Old York Road. BackStreet is third house on left. From New York, take Lincoln Tunnel to New Jersey Turnpike to exit 10. Pick up Route 287 North onto Route 22 West. (Sommerville exit on left) to 202 South to New Hope toll bridge. After toll follow sign into New Hope to traffic light. Make right onto Route 179. Go to MacDonald's and make another left for 1 block, then turn right into Old York Road. BackStreet is third house on left.

WEDGWOOD INN

Where you can learn all about B & B's

The Wedgwood Inn was built on the foundation of "the old hip roof house" where General Alexander, Lord Stirling, stayed during the Revolutionary War. It is therefore fitting that the inn was recently designated to participate in New Hope's celebration of Washington's crossing the Delaware.

Situated two miles from that site, the inn is just four blocks from the center of New Hope. Named after Josiah Wedgwood, many of the inn's rooms have a blue and white theme. An ever-growing collection of Wedgwood porcelain is scattered throughout the house and a whatnot in the parlor displays among other things, a tea set from Queen Elizabeth's coronation, Jasper ware, and a commemorative bicentennial piece.

Guest rooms are comfortably furnished with period pieces. Cubist and Abstract paintings by Nadine's great-aunt combine favorably with a collection of contemporary crafts pieces to create an interesting effect.

In addition to running the inn, Carl and Nadine offer prospective innkeepers week-long seminars in running an inn or bed and breakfast. Everything is covered, from locating and financing a place to checking in guests, and candidates are given an opportunity to test the waters.

Extras at the Wedgwood include breakfast in bed, an afternoon fireside tea, Carl's homemade almond liqueur, and a complimentary ride into town in a Pennsylvania Dutch horse-drawn buggy.

WEDGWOOD INN, 111 West Bridge Street, New Hope, PA 18938; (215) 862-2570; Carl Glassman and Nadine Silnutzer, hosts. Open year-round. Twelve guest rooms including two suites, most with private baths; carriage house with private bath, deck, and kitchenette. Rates: $60-$95 for room with private bath. Inquire for rates on suites and carriage house. Children accepted, call in advance; pets permitted, call in advance; smoking allowed on enclosed back porch; personal checks, travelers checks, cash. Four blocks from center of New Hope.

DIRECTIONS: from I-95 take the New Hope exit and proceed north 10 miles to the center of town. Turn left at the traffic light (only one in town) and continue up hill for 3 blocks. Wedgwood is at top of hill on left.

BRIDGETON HOUSE

French doors onto the Delaware

Bridgeton House sits on the banks of the Delaware River. This is an enviable position, for while many Bucks County hostels advertise proximity to the river as a drawing card, few can truly say the river is their backyard. Beatrice and Charles Briggs restored their seven-room inn with an eye to incorporating the river by installing French doors and laying a pebble patio that sweeps to the edge of the riverbank.

With Charles' talent as a master carpenter and Bea in charge of interior design, the Briggses completely renovated and decorated what was a derelict building, an eyesore caught between the bridge and the road. Today, Bridgeton House feels like a cross between American country-naive and French provincial style. Bea uses soft color throughout, Williamsburg shades of faded cobalt, muted mulberry, and clotted cream. Thick rag rugs and a collection of antique Oriental area rugs accent painted hardwood floors. Fine bed linens and puffy comforters please the eye and assure the traveler of a comfortable night's sleep.

Bridgeton House is a casual, but sophisticated environment. Before becoming innkeepers, Bea and Charles worked in Bucks County inns and restaurants, and their years of experience show. Always available, but never intrusive, Bea sets a relaxing tone. She loves to cook and often can be found in the inn's beautiful kitchen, which opens onto the entry hall and adjoining dining room.

Outside the door, the Delaware River affords many diversions, starting with its lovely sixty-mile towpath, which is perfect for hiking, cross-country skiing, picnicking, and jogging. Canoeing, fishing, and tubing enthusiasts proclaim the Delaware to be among the East Coast's finest rivers.

BRIDGETON HOUSE, River Rd., Upper Black Eddy, PA 18972; (215) 982-5856; Charles and Beatrice Briggs, hosts. Built in 1836 as a private residence, this home also once served as a bakery and candy store. Open year-round. Seven guest rooms, four with river views and balconies, all with private baths. Rates: on weekends by room $70–80, during week $10 less per room; single rate during week $20 less per room. Full breakfast. Good restaurants close by. Children discouraged; no pets; smoking discouraged; personal checks accepted. Swimming, tubing on Delaware River, tow path, fishing, biking, antiques.

DIRECTIONS: from Philadelphia, take I-95 north to New Hope/Yardley exit. Follow signs north to New Hope. Continue north on Rte. 32, 18 miles to inn.

The elegant entry hall.

NEW JERSEY

CHESTNUT HILL ON THE DELAWARE

Old-fashioned and very romantic

Visitors to Linda and Rob Castagna's home, Chestnut Hill, are enveloped by the warmth of the atmosphere and the beauty of the setting on the banks of the Delaware.

Bedrooms are old-fashioned and very romantic, thanks to Linda's gift for color and design and her many small touches. On the door of each room hangs a delicate wreath, and inside a handcrafted cloth basket is filled with fresh fruit in season. One room, entitled Peaches and Cream, is an aptly named chamber with soft peach-striped wallpaper, puffy peach comforter draped with a lace coverlet, and an oak chest of drawers and armoire. The Pineapple Room, which was the servants quarters, is roomy and private at the rear of the second floor. Decorated in cream, yellows,

and greens, the room offers a bed dressed with a luxurious Welsh duvet and a wall of built-in drawers and cabinets in which hides a television. Bayberry features a bay window fitted with original shutters and is decorated in sprightly primary shades taken from colors in the bed's antique quilt.

Up a steep staircase to the attic suite, the bridal favorite, guests are in a world of their own. One bedroom is named Teddy's Place and contains several furry bears and a Little Golden Book of the *Three Bears* tale. Against a warm and rosy red print wallpaper, white eyelet and ruffled bedclothes look crisp and inviting. The bathroom, which displays beautiful Italian tile work, overlooks the swift-flowing Delaware.

CHESTNUT HILL ON THE DELAWARE, 63 Church St., Milford, NJ 08848; (201) 995-9761; Linda and Rob Castagna, hosts. Victorian house built in 1860, with gallery/gift shop on premises. Open year-round. Five guest rooms, shared and private baths. Rates: $60 to $80 singles, $120 suite. Full breakfast served. Excellent dining in area. No pets; no smoking; checks accepted.

DIRECTIONS: from Milford, turn right at light and right again on Church St. (1 street before Delaware River bridge). Turn left into dead-end, which is Chestnut Hill's parking area.

Left, a photograph of the hosts and their son, dressed in the period clothes that they love to collect.

WHIMSEY HALL

Country comfort

Jean and Ernie Borden were indulging a whim when they bought this pre-Civil War three-story brick Federal farmhouse in Burlington County, the largest county in New Jersey, which stretches from Trenton to the sea. Acknowledging that the house was advantageously situated between the shore and pine barrens and Pennsylvania's Bucks County, the newly retired couple began plotting the building's renewal. Using family antiques and such treasures from the Northeast as an Amish pew in the front hall and an outhouse from a local church in the fern grotto out back, the Bordens have created a feeling of whimsical country comfort. Although modern malls are a short drive away, so are public halls that sponsor oyster roasts, turkey dinners, and Saturday auctions.

WHIMSEY HALL. Circa 1845 brick farmhouse on seven acres surrounded by 250 acres of farmland. Open all year. Three guest rooms with shared bath; one room with fireplace; private bath available on request; air conditioning. Rates: $55 single; $65 double. Full breakfast served indoors by the fire, in bed, or at table. No pets. *Represented by Bed & Breakfast of Philadelphia.*

Breakfast anyone?

WOOLVERTON INN

A grand setting near Bucks County

The two most striking characteristics of the Woolverton Inn are its grand situation and the relaxed and flexible atmosphere. The building is a large and impressive manor house of undressed stone; the original section was built around 1793, and the mansard-roofed third floor, decorative iron grillwork, and long sweeping porches were added in 1876.

The setting is lovely. Fully grown sugar maples stand like sentinels in the sweeping front lawn, and in autumn their foliage is breathtakingly brilliant. Behind the house, sheep graze on the rolling meadow that stretches as far as the eye can see. The grounds are spacious enough to feel isolated from the world, though the inn is quite close to the village of Stockton.

The furnishings of the house—a fine selection of antiques and assorted comfortable easy chairs and sofas—blend compatibly with the elegance of the formal dining room, the rusticity of wide-plank oak floors and narrow hallways.

Woolverton emanates an easy-going attitude of laissez-faire. This tone is exemplified in the breakfast regimen. Guests may take this meal when they want and where they want, be it in their room at 7 A.M. or under a maple tree at 3 P.M. On Sunday morning a brunch can feature cheese omelets, poached eggs, or French toast and sausage.

Horse shoes, croquet, and bocci ball are played on the expansive lawn. There is an abundance of wildlife here to satisfy both animal lovers and birders.

WOOLVERTON INN, Box 233, R.D. 3, Stockton, NJ 08559: (609) 397-0802; David Salassie, Host. French spoken. Gracious colonial stone manor house on ten acres of land. Open year-round. Ten rooms in manor house sharing 5 baths; one suite in carriage house with private bath. Rates: $50 to 100. Full continental breakfast, afternoon tea. Excellent dining in area. No children under fourteen; no pets; Visa/MasterCard/checks. Endless possibilities for recreation in scenic Bucks County.

DIRECTIONS: from Philadelphia, take I-95 north and cross Delaware River to N.J. Take first exit in N.J. (Rte. 29) and follow 29 north through Lambertville to Stockton. Take Rte. 523 for ⅛ mile and turn left on Woolverton Rd. Inn is second drive on right. From New York City, take N.J. Tnpke. south to Exit 10. Then take Rte. 287 north for 14 miles to Rte. 22 exit west. Continue on 22 for 2½ miles and take Rte. 202 exit south for 25 miles to Lambertville exit just before Delaware River Bridge. Take Rte. 29 north to Stockton.

YORK STREET HOUSE

The most formal and elegant of all

Because it was built by a wealthy coal magnate as a lavish anniversary gift for his wife, the York Street House is one of the most formal and elegant inns in the Bucks County area. George Massey spared no expense and in 1909 spent $65,000 on his home. On the first floor he installed three beautiful Mercer tile fireplaces—one in the formal parlor, one in the dining room, and a third in the cherrywood-paneled library. Leaded glass wall cases, colorful stained-glass windows, and a Waterford crystal chandelier were a few of the elegant details. The second floor was given over to bedchambers and dressing rooms for the Masseys, and servants quarters and a sewing room occupied the third floor. Such was the spending and splendor of the house, that *House and Garden* magazine featured the Massey Mansion in its December 1911 issue.

The Teddy Roosevelt Room.

Before its life as an inn, the house was used as a designer showcase. One of the more interesting and successful designs—a bedroom decorated with tiny leopard-spot cloth wallcovering, a Victorian bedroom set painted the buttery shades of tans and browns, an elegant checked wool quilt, and pinstriped sheeting—is atypical, masculine in feel, and goes by the name Teddy Roosevelt. More typical are the bedrooms dressed in Laura Ashley prints that create a light and charming mood. Each of the third-floor bedrooms has that cozy feeling that sloping ceilings and dormer windows give to any space.

The downstairs parlor is a soft mix of palest lavender walls accented by white moldings and furnishings in shades of green and rose. A selection of small oil paintings adorn the walls, and the Waterford chandelier hangs in its original spot. Across the hall the dark cherrywood depths of the library play a contrasting role.

YORK STREET HOUSE, 42 York St., Lambertville, NJ 08530; (609) 397-3007; Gladys Herschel, host. Georgian Revival home built in 1909. Open year-round. Seven guest rooms, shared and private baths. Rates: $65 to $75. Full breakfast served. Excellent dining in area. No children under twelve; no pets; checks accepted. All the pleasures of Bucks County.

DIRECTIONS: from Philadelphia, take I-95 north and cross Delaware River. Take Lambertville exit (Rte. 29) north to York St. and turn left.

ASHLING COTTAGE

Beautifully preserved

Guests arriving at Ashling Cottage in any season will discover a hospitable, delightful respite from the workaday world. Using bold Victorian colors and a mix of oak and contemporary furnishings, goodi and Jack Stewart carry the feel of the Victorian age into the age of modern comforts.

Most of the ten guest rooms are cozy and spacious. The green and neutral hued room number 3 is a bath-lover's delight with three steps down to a large claw-foot tub. The bathroom's hexagonal tiles and pedestal sink further create an air of old-fashioned luxury. But the most asked-after room is the hideaway with the separate entrance, where lace and ruffles predominate among Laura Ashley pinks and greens.

ASHLING COTTAGE, 106 Sussex Ave., Spring Lake, NJ 07762; (201) 449-3553; Jack and goodi Stewart, hosts. Open March through December. German spoken. Ten guest rooms, eight with private baths. Rates: $65 to $95; cots, $15; includes continental breakfast. Children under 12 discouraged; no pets; smoking on first floor only; no credit cards. Passes to private beach. Will meet guests at bus or train.

DIRECTIONS: from the Garden State Parkway, take exit 98 and head south on Rte. 34 to the traffic circle; at the circle head east on Rte. 547 for approximately 3 miles to First Ave. Turn right onto First Ave., then right again onto Sussex Ave. Ashling Cottage is the second house on the right.

THE KENILWORTH

Bed, breakfast, and boardwalk

Like a grand dame who lets her hair gray, the Kenilworth shows its age engagingly. The twenty-three bedrooms, almost all with outstanding water views, are simply furnished and designed for swimmers with wet suits and sandy footsteps.

Co-host Debbie Czajko (pronounced Chi-ko) affably presides over the living and television room, attending to guests' needs by offering homemade iced tea and lemonade on summer evenings out on the breezy porch or amid the hanging plants indoors. She also makes sure that everyone has helped themselves to the ample cold breakfast buffet, which includes a fresh fruit cup and homemade muffins.

The Kenilworth attracts a casual crowd, and bicycles, surfboards, beach chairs, and umbrellas can all be rented at the front desk. This is a place to put your feet up and relax—a beach home with the roaring ocean only a few steps past the boardwalk.

THE KENILWORTH, 1505 Ocean Ave., Spring Lake, NJ 07762; (201) 449-5327; Bob and Debbie Czajko, hosts. Some Spanish spoken. Open all year. Twenty-three guest rooms, thirteen with private bath. Rates: $35 to $39, single, in season; $50 to $82, double, in season. Off-season discounts range from 20% to 30% off. Additional person in room, $12; children under five, free; no pets; MasterCard/Visa. Tennis; golf; fishing saltwater pools; horseback riding nearby. Special English Weekends a house specialty.

DIRECTIONS: take exit 98 off the Garden State Parkway. Head south on Rte. 34 to the traffic circle; at the circle, head east on Rte. 524 (Allaire Rd.), which leads to Ocean Ave. Turn right at the ocean; the house is 4½ blocks up on the right.

The largest, most imposing guest room.

THE NORMANDY INN

Gracious privacy a block from the beach

Of all the seaside villages that attract vacationers to the New Jersey shore, none is more gracious than Spring Lake. Bypassed by the teeming hordes who populate streets, casinos, and beaches of larger resorts, Spring Lake emanates a special grace particular to communities made up of broad avenues lined with grand, tree-shaded "cottages."

Built in 1888 as a private residence and expanded in 1916, The Normandy Inn, which comprises twenty bedrooms, sits one block from the beach. Size alone makes the Normandy feel like a small resort hotel, though innkeepers Susan and Michael Ingino, who live in the house year-round with daughter Beth, maintain a warm and homey atmosphere.

Breakfast at this inn is especially generous and delicious. Each morning guests seat themselves in the large dining room—a room of such scale that young Beth dreams of converting it into her own private skating rink. The written menu offers many choices. Besides the requisite juices, hot beverages, and cold cereals, the Inginos serve real Irish porridge, four types of pancakes, two sorts of French toast, six varieties of eggs, four breakfast meats, and Michael's fresh-baked muffins or soda bread. Breakfast is Michael's favorite meal, and as a chef, he sees to it that guests need eat but a sparing lunch.

The Inginos are avid collectors of Victoriana and have almost completed furnishing each room with antiques and details from the period. Rooms vary in size, but each is clean and very comfortable.

THE NORMANDY INN, 21 Tuttle Ave., Spring Lake, NJ 07762; (201) 449-7172; Michael and Susan Ingino, hosts. Italianate Victorian home near beach offers casual comfort and thoughtful amenities. Open all year. Eighteen guest rooms in house, two over garage, most with private baths. Rates $55 to $95 in season, $50 to $75 off season, double occupancy. Includes full breakfast. Good dining throughout area. Children who enjoy quietude welcome; no pets; smoking discouraged; no credit cards. Area offers beach, horseback riding, antiques, state park.

DIRECTIONS: from north, take Garden State Pkwy. to exit 98 (Rte. 34). Proceed south on 34 to traffic circle. Drive ¾ way around and turn right on Rte. 524 east. Cross Rtes. 35 and 71. Rte. 524 then becomes Ludlow Ave. Proceed to end of Ludlow and turn right onto Ocean Ave., then first right onto Tuttle. From south, take Garden State Pkwy. to exit 98 (Rte. 38 E). Cross Rte. 18 and turn right at next traffic light onto New Bedford Rd. Take sharp left at second stop sign (Rte. 524) and proceed as above.

CONOVER'S BAY HEAD INN

The pearl of seaside inns

Beverly Conover's light touch and delicate sense of color reveal an exquisite aesthetic sensitivity that defines the inn—from the embracing warm tones of lavender and mauve on the first floor to the family photographs she has framed and placed in each room.

Every one of the twelve dignified bedrooms has a distinct personality. The brightest room is also the most dramatic. Splashes of red and green in the geranium wallpaper match the brilliant red of the table skirt and ruffled cushion on the white wicker settee. In another room, a smoke-blue and white Laura Ashley print on the wall is reversed on the chair upholstery. In yet another, a spool bed and curly maple dresser are paired with pink and lime linens, a green stenciled border, and a row of small porcelain ducks that nest on top of the window sill.

The views are equally impressive. The sinuously curved maple bed in one third-floor room is placed so that reclining guests can see the bay, marina, and yacht club. Reflections of the ocean gleam in other rooms. Shapely old-style shingle houses comprise the rest of the scenic landscape.

Bay Head captures the feel of a late nineteenth-century residential summer village. The few, quaint shops sell antiques, art wear, prints, books, gifts, and clothing. Very little tells of life's more pressing necessities. "Which is as it should be," notes Beverly.

"I like to fuss. I always fuss over breakfast," Beverly adds. Inspired baked goods grace the table as beautifully as the place settings. Fresh-squeezed orange juice and cut fruit appear on the table every day, and on Sunday Beverly prepares a tasty egg dish. Guests can dine in the sunny breakfast room, on the manicured lawn, or on the front porch.

Conover's is a classic among bed and breakfasts, the pearl of seaside inns.

CONOVER'S BAY HEAD INN, 646 Main Ave., Bay Head, NJ 08742; (201) 892-4664; Carl and Beverly Conover, hosts. Open February 15 to December 15. Summer cottage built in 1912 and located one block from the beach. Twelve guest rooms; six second-story guest rooms have private baths; six third-story rooms share two baths. Rates: $55 to $100 in season; off-season discounts; $20 for additional person; singles $5 to $10 less double rate. Light breakfast included. Tea served in the afternoons until May 1. Children aged 13 and up are welcome in July and August only; no pets; limited smoking; American Express/MasterCard/Visa. Lawn games; golf; tennis; winter sports on Twilight Lake; beach; windsurfing.

DIRECTIONS: from the Garden State Parkway, take Rte. 34 (exit 98) and follow signs for Rte. 35. Continue on Rte. 35 south into Bay Head. The inn is on the right.

Left, Joy Peto Smiley, John Peto's granddaughter, in the studio. Above, some of John Peto's paintings, including a self-portrait on the easel.

THE STUDIO OF JOHN F. PETO

A secluded artist's studio

Gifted in the art of still life, John F. Peto, who lived during the latter half of the nineteenth century, was an artist whose talent was to go unrecognized in his lifetime. Throughout his career, he was unfavorably compared to friend and fellow painter William Michael Harnett. In 1950 the tide began to turn when the Brooklyn Museum mounted Peto's first major exhibition. Thirty-three years later when the National Gallery of Art organized a retrospective that traveled from Washington, D.C. to the Amon Carter Museum in Fort Worth, Texas, Peto finally emerged as a major American painter, now considered by many to be a far greater talent than Harnett.

Peto lived his life in virtual seclusion in Island Heights, a quiet village along the New Jersey shore, in a house he built overlooking the Tom's River. He first designed a studio for himself, a spacious and high-ceilinged room with white stuccoed fireplace, white walls, and "Peto red" wainscoting. He then built his home, including seven bedrooms, around the studio.

Granddaughter Joy Peto Smiley, as ebullient as her forebears were reclusive, has opened her grandfather's home and studio to overnight guests. Rooms are furnished much as they always have been, unpretentious with an eclectic mix of beds, chest, and chairs. In the common rooms hang reproductions of Peto's most famous paintings, and the studio holds a small selection of his original works.

Whether dining on Joy's "ethereal eggs," fresh fruit, and hot popovers, or walking through historic Island Heights, the studio, filled with the strong and quiet presence of John Peto, is the most memorable part of a stay.

THE STUDIO OF JOHN F. PETO, 102 Cedar Ave., Island Heights, NJ 08732; (201) 270-6058; Joy Peto Smiley, hostess. Open year-round. Seven guest rooms, shared baths. Rates: $35 to $75. Hearty breakfast served. Variety of restaurants, including a wonderful seafood eatery, in the area. No children; no pets; Visa/MasterCard/American Express/checks.

DIRECTIONS: take Garden State Pkwy. to exit 82 east. Pass through six stoplights. Two blocks further, turn right onto Central Ave. and drive ¼ mile; halfway up the first hill, turn left onto Summit. Drive 4 blocks and turn right onto Cedar. Inn is 2 blocks on left (look for sign "The Studio").

Left, the dining room, furnished in impeccable Victorian style.

THE MAINSTAY INN

Bed and breakfast at its best

The heyday of Cape May as one of the premier resort towns on the East Coast coincided with the height of Victorian carpenter craftsmanship in the latter part of the nineteenth century, and Cape May has hundreds of finely crafted, exquisitely detailed gingerbread houses to prove it.

One of these, an Italianate former gaming house built in 1872, was restored to its former glory by Tom and Sue Carroll, who have made the Mainstay into the best known bed and breakfast in the East. Because of their painstaking search for authenticity in the recreation of Victorian interiors, their inn has become a highly respected and much-loved model for other innkeepers aspiring to recreate the same sort of ambiance.

The interior of the inn is a unique combination of lush, Persian and Oriental rugs, wonderfully decorative Bradbury and Bradbury period wallpapers and mouldings, elaborate details in the form of paintings, china, drapes, lamps, quilts, chandeliers, clocks, vases, and, finally, an overwhelming collection of Victorian antique furniture. Guest rooms contain giant beds with decorative foot and head boards, intricately carved wardrobes, dressers, and washstands with marble tops, and velvet upholstered chairs and settees. The public rooms contain more: giant pier mirrors, elaborately upholstered walnut and mahogany chairs and settees, and exotic divans.

Amidst this Victorian flamboyance, the perfectly modern young innkeepers maintain an air of calm and serenity throughout the two guest houses. Guests meet each other over the delicious full breakfasts and during afternoon tea, oftentimes served on the Mainstay's ample porch.

THE MAINSTAY INN, 635 Columbia Avenue, Cape May, NJ 08204; (609) 884-8690; Tom and Sue Carroll, hosts. Open April through November. Thirteen rooms, nine with private baths, four sharing two baths. Rates: $70 to $85 per couple in season; includes full breakfast and afternoon tea. No liquor served; guests may bring their own. Children over 12 welcome; no pets; smoking on veranda only; no credit cards. Croquet and swimming at the seashore are popular activities.

DIRECTIONS: 2 blocks from Convention Hall in the center of town.

Cape May is the nation's oldest seaside resort, and a stroll along its tree-lined, gaslit streets at dusk on a summer's evening recreates the heyday of the nineteenth century: ice cream parlors, Sousa brass bands, bicycles, carriages, knickered boys, hoops, and mustachioed U.S. Presidents looking on as frequent visitors.

At the center of everything is The Chalfont, a wondrous construction in decorative wood that also serves great meals; perfect for all the visitors to Cape May staying at bed and breakfast inns. The backdrop to it all is the incredible collection of hundreds of extravagantly ornamented Victorian houses built in Italianate and Gothic Revival styles, among which The Abbey stands out.

THE ABBEY, Columbia Avenue and Gurney Street, Cape May, NJ 08204; (609) 884-4506; Jay and Marianne Schatz, hosts. Open April through November. Seven rooms, four with private baths and three sharing one large bath. Rates: $58 to $88 per couple; includes full breakfast in spring and fall, lighter buffet in summer, and afternoon refreshments through the year, and on-site parking. No liquor served; guests may bring their own. Well-behaved children over 12 welcome; no pets; all smoking limited to the veranda; Visa/MasterCard/American Express. Croquet at the inn, seashore swimming one block away, and many other activities.

DIRECTIONS: in Cape May, turn left on Ocean street, drive 3 blocks and turn left on Columbia Avenue. The inn is one block down.

THE ABBEY

Casual elegance

One of the more elaborate carpenter gothic houses in Cape May is a seaside "cottage" built in 1869 by a wealthy coal baron who spared no expense in creating an architectural masterpiece for entertaining summer guests at the sea shore. Now transformed into a bed and breakfast of expansive proportions by Jay and Marianne Schatz, the building has been delightfully restored. The interior contains a variety of decorative Victorian wallpaper reproductions as a setting for a collection of nineteenth-century furniture and bric-a-brac that brings the period back to life in a charming way.

Croquet on the lawn, with the men wearing straw boaters; afternoon tea on the porch, including the hosts leading stimulating conversation with the guests; music played on an antique harp or an 1850 square grand piano in the parlor, which functions essentially as a music room; all these add to the atmosphere of life in another time—less hurried, less hectic, less harrowing.

Left, everyone enjoys croquet as much as porch sitting. Above, a tour de force of Victorian decoration.

CAPTAIN MEY'S INN

Graced with exquisite detail

America's oldest seaside resort, Cape May conjures by its very name, visions of gingerbread and wedding-cake castles-by-the-sea. Protected from progress by the Pine Barrens and acres of wetlands plus miles of fertile fields that yield succulent Jersey produce, the village retains much of the charm of centuries past.

One advantage for today's visitor is the abundance of lovely bed and breakfast establishments, each quite different in spirit and temperament. The three on these pages are a sampler; it would take weeks to exhaust all the possibilities.

Captain Mey's Inn is named for Cornelius Jacobsen Mey, of the Dutch East Indies Company, who explored the area in 1621 and served as its namesake. This solidly built, late-Victorian mansion is decorated like an old-fashioned valentine. Voluminous lace curtains and lacey privacy screens,

Two details of the foyer and parlor.

called *horretjes*, frame the windows. A china cabinet filled with innkeeper Carin Fedderman's collection of antique Delftware, family portraits, a nineteenth-century bible, antique pewter and copper, and abundant knickknacks and bric-a-brac fill the first-floor parlor and dining room. Carin is from Holland, and her Dutch heritage, linked with that of Captain Mey, inspired her and partner Milly La Canfora to create an inn reminiscent of her home. Many small touches—a small Persian rug on the clawfoot dining table; a plush, purse-like tea cozy; and the decorative *horretjes*—are found in many Dutch homes and add a distinctive European flavor. The house itself is graced with exquisite detail from three signed Tiffany stained-glass windows in the inner foyer to leaded, diamond-paned, ripple glass windows that glisten in the wide bay in the dining room.

CAPTAIN MEY'S INN, 202 Ocean St., Cape May, NJ 08204; (609) 884-7793/9637; Carin Fedderman and Milly La Canfora, hostesses. Dutch spoken and some French, German, Spanish, Italian. Open all year. Eight guest rooms, private and shared baths. Rates $65 to $90 double, varying with season and amenities; includes full breakfast served by candlelight. Afternoon tea. Excellent dining nearby. No children under twelve; no pets; smoking restricted to the veranda; Visa/MasterCard; parking available. Cape May offers beaches (beach passes available), sight-seeing, antiques.

DIRECTIONS: take causeway bridge (Lafayette St.) to second light and turn left onto Ocean St. Inn is 1½ blocks ahead.

A Dutch tea cozy.

THE QUEEN VICTORIA

Imposing Victorian on Cape May

The Queen Victoria ranks among the best of Cape May's many distinctive bed and breakfast inns. It towers on the corner of Ocean Street and Columbia Avenue, a dramatic green and maroon gingerbread cottage. Owners Joan and Dane Wells are perfectly suited to the task of pampering this Victorian lady. Before beginning a career as an innkeeper, Joan was curator of the Molly Brown House in Denver as well as the executive director of The Victorian Society. Both positions required a dedication to the preservation of old houses, a labor Joan truly loves. Dan is the perfect counterpart. Though a tinkerer and hardware store aficionado, his professional background in retailing keeps the inn's business side on an even keel.

One of the most attractive and interesting rooms in the entire house is the front parlor, which is filled with the Wellses' Arts and Crafts furniture collection—that wonderfully subdued offspring of the gaudy Victorian age.

Bedrooms come in many shapes and sizes. On the first floor the Queen Victoria room handily houses a massive armoire, tufted couch, king-size bed, and petit point chairs. Several rooms on the second floor and all on the third are diminutive and charming. The Wellses carefully selected wallpapers to suit the spirit of Victoriana, each with jewel-like hues and intricate patterns.

Though Cape May is a wonderful place to visit, no matter the season, the Wellses favorite time of year is Christmas. To make the season more joyous, they organize caroling, fireside readings from Dickens, and workshop sessions devoted to planning the Victorian Christmas dinner and decorating the Victorian home.

THE QUEEN VICTORIA, 102 Ocean St., Cape May, NJ 08204; (609) 884-8702; Dane and Joan Wells, hosts. French and some Spanish spoken. Open all year, minimum stays vary seasonally. Twelve guest rooms, private and shared baths. Rates: $52 to $100 according to size and amenities (rates lower off season), including full breakfast served buffet style. Afternoon tea. Excellent dining nearby. No toddlers; no pets; smoking restricted; Visa/MasterCard.

DIRECTIONS: take Garden State Pkwy. to Cape May, where it becomes Lafayette St. Turn left at second stoplight (Ocean St.) and proceed three blocks to inn, on right.

MARYLAND

Stay the night in a comfortable museum

Three and one half years of preparation went into the making of the White Swan Tavern, and the effect is that of a comfortable museum. The original section of the building dates back to the early 1700s when John Lovegrove operated a tannery on the site. Over the years the property changed hands and became a tavern that offered accommodations to travelers. In 1977, Horace Havemeyer, Jr., bought the property. Before beginning the restoration, he undertook exhaustive historical research and an archeological dig. Artifacts and shards of pottery, including a serving dish (a 1730 North Devon charger) that has been beautifully reproduced as the inn's china, are on display in a backlit wall case.

A stay at the White Swan is rewarding because guests can feel the care the inn has been given. The main floor contains three parlors, or sitting rooms. The formal and dignified Joseph Nicholson Room, named after the second owner of the property, is furnished from Mr. Nicholson's inventory, a document unearthed during research. The Isaac Cannell Room is filled with game tables appropriate to the days when it was an integral part of the original tavern.

Bedrooms are decorated in several styles. Three are done in formal colonial: one with pencil post twin beds, one with a lace canopied double bed, and one with cannonball four-posters. All have wing chairs for reading, fresh colors, and beautiful hardwood floors. The T.W. Elliason Suite, added to the tavern at the turn-of-the-century, has been restored to its Victorian origins. This bedroom and separate sitting room are decorated with high-back massive beds, a tufted settee, decorative friezes, and a busy floral carpet. A unique color scheme of golds, greens, copper, and peach is vibrant and true to the era. The final bedchamber is located in the oldest section of the structure. Named Lovegrove's Kitchen because it was the site of its namesake's tannery, this rustic suite has an original beam ceiling, brick floor, wide

Above, the old kitchen serves as a guest room.

The King Joseph Room, a private sitting room for guests, above.

In the winter the inn is filled with dried flowers.

kitchen hearth, and is accented with homespun blue-and-cream curtains and bedspreads, antique tables, and a wing chair for reading.

The White Swan's continental breakfast is special because it employs the talents of a gifted local baker and includes fresh-squeezed orange juice and grapefruit juice. Served in the Isaac Cannell Room, guests may request that breakfast be delivered to their door instead.

Chestertown, an important seaport in the early 1700s, is one of those special American towns that still reflects its moment of prosperity. The seat of Kent County and the home of Washington College, the town retains a great measure of grace and atmosphere.

WHITE SWAN TAVERN, 231 High St., Chestertown, MD 21620; (301) 778-2300; Mary S. Clarkson, hostess. Closed two weeks per year (usually early February). Five guest rooms in house, one attached "summer kitchen" suite, all private baths. Rates: $75 to $90, double occupancy; $25 per extra occupant; rates include light breakfast. Good dining nearby, especially in season. Children welcome; no pets; no credit cards. Area offers local museums, walking tours, recreation, wildlife preserves.

DIRECTIONS: from Chesapeake Bay Bridge (Rte. 50-301), take Rte. 301N to Rte. 213. Turn left on Rte. 213 to Chestertown, approx. 15 miles. Cross the Chester River Bridge and turn left at first stop light (Cross St.). Turn left again at next light (High St.). Inn is in middle of block on right. From north, take Rte. 301S to Rte. 544. Proceed on 544 to stop light and turn left. Pass college and turn right at second light (Cross St.) Proceed as above.

Top left, the guests' billiard room in the contemporary townhouse. Bottom left, the guest room in the historic Annapolis home. Above, one of a fleet of bed and breakfast boats.

ANNAPOLIS

Living history with bed and breakfast

Annapolis resonates a quiet charm that reflects its deep sense of history. At the confluence of the Severn River and Chesapeake Bay, its setting is captivating. Narrow, crooked streets lined with brick sidewalks and old houses—more than sixty of which are pre-Revolutionary structures—lead toward the historic waterfront, where a forest of boat masts gently bob and wave. Between 1750 and 1780, Annapolis experienced its Golden Age. During those years the town built both the first library and the first theater in the colonies as well as the Maryland State House, the oldest state capitol in the United States in continuous use. It was here, too, in 1783, that General George Washington resigned his commission as commander-in-chief of the Continental Army, and, in 1784, that the Treaty of Paris was signed, officially ending the American Revolution.

The three bed and breakfast residences pictured are a varied sampler of those available in the Annapolis area. Just outside of town, one host family offers visitors the entire first floor of their contemporary townhouse, which includes a billiard room with working fireplace and color television, and an immaculate bedroom and bath. Another home, found in the center of Annapolis, is within walking distance of most of the town's historic sites and great little restaurants and bistros. As an added bonus, this house has a lovely swimming pool in its backyard.

Visitors with a nautical bent may stay aboard one of many large boats docked in the Chesapeake or downtown Annapolis.

MOTOR YACHT . Sleeps four. One of fifty motor and sailing yachts docked in downtown Annapolis, Baltimore's Inner Harbor, and the Eastern Shore that are available for bed and breakfast from April 15 to Oct. 15. Rates: 34 footers and up, from $75 double. *Represented by The Traveller in Maryland, Annapolis, MD.*

CONTEMPORARY TOWNHOUSE . Open year-round. One guest room, private bath, and billiard room. Rates: $45 single, $65 double. Continental breakfast, full breakfast on weekends. No children; no pets. *Represented by Sweet Dreams & Toast, Inc., Washington, DC.*

HISTORIC DISTRICT . An Annapolis "vernacular" house open year-round. One guest room, private bath. Rates for double occupancy: $55. Full breakfast. Small pets only; smoking discouraged. *Represented by The Traveller in Maryland, Annapolis, MD.*

One of the restored parlors.

SPRING BANK INN

The rebirth of a stylish rural home

In 1880 gentleman farmer George Houck spared no expense when he built the most stylish home rural Frederick County had ever seen. Constructed of red brick, the house was given a Gothic Revival bay window, columned veranda, and gabled, fish-scale patterned slate roof. It was further embellished with elegant Italianate windows and an ornate belvedere for viewing the beautiful vistas of the surrounding countryside.

A century later the house captured the imaginations of Beverly and Ray Compton, who noticed it while on a bicycle tour of the area. Captivated as well by the rich history and architectural charms of Frederick, they soon bought Spring Bank Farm and embarked on a massive and much-needed restoration. Since the Comptons open bedrooms to overnight guests as each room is completed, today's guests are attending the birth of an inn and the rebirth of a house, with such fine details as frescoed ceilings, original brass hardware, louvered shutters, hand-marbled slate fireplaces, and hand-grained woodwork revealing themselves in the process.

Ray's family has been in the antiques business for several decades, and this expertise shows in many of Spring Bank's furnishings. High-ceilinged bedrooms easily accommodate full Victorian bedroom sets, canopied beds, and easy chairs. Plans are in the works to convert the third floor, which gives access to the belvedere, into an antiques shop.

SPRING BANK INN, 7945 Worman's Mill Rd., Frederick, MD 21701; (301) 694-0440; Beverly and Ray Compton, hosts. Elegant 1880 rural home that combines Greek Revival and Italiante architecture. Open year-round. Seven guest rooms, one with private bath. Rates $50–60 single, $60–75 double. Hearty continental breakfast. No children under twelve; no pets; no smoking in home; American Express/checks. Appalachian trail close by; trout fishing; historic district to explore. Wide range of good restaurants in town.

DIRECTIONS: from I-70, I-270, or 340, take U.S. 15 north about 5 miles, driving past Frederick. Look for "mile 16" marker; turn right at next road onto Rte. 355 south. Inn is ¼ mile south on left.

BED & BREAKFAST RESERVATION AGENCIES

The concept of Bed and Breakfast in the United States is rapidly expanding. To facilitate this phenomenon, reservation agencies are quickly cropping up, resulting in rapidly changing information. Many of the agencies listed below have been in existence for some time; others have been organized recently. Do not be surprised if there are changes when you contact them.

*Only a selection of agencies are listed here. Complete information can be obtained from **Bed and Breakfast Reservation Services Worldwide**, P.O. Box 14797, Dept 174, Baton Rouge, LA 70898.*

Connecticut

BED AND BREAKFAST, LTD., P.O. Box 216, New Haven, CT 06513; (203) 469-3260; Jack Argenio. Write, sending SASE, or call between 5–9 P.M. weekdays and any time weekends. Period homes, estates, farms. *125 listings statewide.*

COVERED BRIDGE BED & BREAKFAST, P.O. Box 701, Norfolk, CT 06058; (203) 542-5944; Diane Trembay. *Northwest Connecticut, southern Berkshires,* Hudson Valley.

NUTMEG BED AND BREAKFAST AGENCY, 222 Girard Avenue, Hartford, CT 06105; (203) 236-6698; Maxine Kates. 9 A.M. to 5 P.M. Monday through Friday. Vacation homes, restored historic homes, relocation. *Connecticut.*

Delaware

BED AND BREAKFAST OF DELAWARE, 3650 Silverside Rd., Box 177, Wilmington, DE 19810; (302) 479-9500; Bette Reese. *Delaware and nearby Pennsylvania and Maryland.*

District of Columbia

THE BED & BREAKFAST LEAGUE, LTD., 3639 Van Ness Street, N.W., Washington, DC 20008; (202) 363-7767; Millie Groobey. *Washington, D.C., Annapolis, Baltimore, New York, San Francisco.*

BED 'N' BREAKFAST LTD. OF WASHINGTON, D.C., P.O. Box 12011, Washington, DC 20005; (202) 328-3510; Jackie Reed and Lisa Stofan. *Washington metropolitan areas, specializing in the historic districts.*

SWEET DREAMS & TOAST, INC., P.O. Box 4835-0035, Washington, DC 20008; (202) 483-9191; Ellie Chastain. *District of Columbia and greater Washington.*

Maine

BED & BREAKFAST DOWN EAST LTD., Macomber Mill Road, Box 547, Eastbrook, ME 04634; (207) 565-3517; Sally Godfrey. Private homes at lakeside, countryside, town, or coast. *Maine.*

BED & BREAKFAST OF MAINE, 32 Colonial Village, Falmouth, ME 04105; (207) 781-4528; Peg Tierney. Weekdays 6–11 P.M.; weekends 10 A.M. to 10 P.M. *Coastal Maine and nearby islands.*

Maryland

THE TRAVELLER IN MARYLAND, 33 West Street, Annapolis, MD 21401; (301) 269-6232, 261-2233; Cecily Sharp-Whitehill. 9 A.M. to 5 P.M. Monday to Thursday; 9 A.M. to noon Friday. Yachts, inns, private homes. *Maryland, London, Paris.*

Massachusetts

BED AND BREAKFAST ASSOCIATES, Bay Colony, Ltd., P.O. Box 166, Babson Park Branch, Boston, MA 02157; (617) 449-5302; Arline Kardasis. *Eastern Massachusetts.*

BED AND BREAKFAST BROOKLINE/BOSTON, Box 732, Brookline, MA 02146; (617) 277-2292; Anne Diamond. 10 A.M. to 4 P.M. Victorian townhouses and Beacon Hill homes. *Boston/Brookline, Cambridge, Cape Cod, Nantucket, Plymouth, Gloucester.*

BED AND BREAKFAST A LÀ CAMBRIDGE AND GREATER BOSTON, 73 Kirkland Street, Cambridge, MA 02138; (617) 576-1492; Riva Poor. 9 A.M. to 6 P.M. Monday–Friday; 2 P.M. to 5 P.M. Saturday. Upper middleclass, vacation, and Share-A-Homes. *Boston, Cambridge, Cape Cod, Martha's Vineyard, Block Island, and Nantucket.*

BED AND BREAKFAST CAPE COD, Box 341, West Hyannisport, MA 02672; (617) 775-2772; Clark and Joyce Diehl. Country inns, sea captains' houses, host homes. *Cape Cod only.*

BERKSHIRE BED AND BREAKFAST HOMES, P.O. Box 211, Williamsburg, MA 01096; (413) 268-7244; Eleanor Hebert. *Private homes in western Mass. from Sturbridge to the Berkshires.*

HOST HOMES OF BOSTON, P.O. Box 117, Newton, MA 02168; (617) 244-1308; Marcia Whittington. *Covers Boston and select city suburbs.*

PINEAPPLE HOSPITALITY, INC., 384 Rodney French Blvd., New Bedford, MA 02744; (617) 990-1696; Joan Brownhill. 9 A.M. to 6 P.M. weekdays. Homes or small inns. *Six-state area of New England.*

New Hampshire

NEW HAMPSHIRE BED & BREAKFAST, RFD 3, Box 53, Laconia, NH 03246; (603) 279-8348; Martha Dorais. Country classics, waterfront, mountain views, farms. *New Hampshire.*

New Jersey

BED & BREAKFAST OF NEW JERSEY, INC., Suite 132, 103 Godwin Avenue, Midland Park, NJ 07432; (201) 444-7409; Aster Mould. Vacation homes, refurbished mansions, apartments. *New Jersey, including seashore area.*

New York

ALTERNATE LODGINGS INC., P.O. Box 1782, East Hampton, L.I., NY 11937; (516) 324-9449; Francine and Robert Hauxwell. *The Hamptons from Westhampton to Montauk Point.*

THE AMERICAN COUNTRY COLLECTION, 984 Gloucester Place, Schenectady, NY 12309; (518) 370-4948; Beverly Walsh. *Northeastern New York, Vermont, Western Massachusetts.*

A REASONABLE ALTERNATIVE, INC., 117 Spring Street, Port Jefferson, NY 11777; (516) 928-4034; Kathleen Dexter. *Long Island along the North and South shores of Nassau and Suffolk Counties.*

BED AND BREAKFAST (& BOOKS), 35 West 92nd Street, New York, NY 10025; (212) 865-8740; Stanley Lewis. A unique service offering a selection of hosts who work as photographers, psychologists, lawyers, dancers, teachers, and artists, with special knowledge of New York's rich cultural life. *New York City.*

THE B & B GROUP (NEW YORKERS AT HOME) INC., 301 E. 60th Street, New York, NY 10022; (212) 838-7015; Farla Zammit. Host homes from brownstones to high-rises. *New York City.*

BED & BREAKFAST U.S.A., LTD., 129 Grand Street, Croton-on-Hudson, NY 10520; (914) 271-6228; Barbara Notarius and Doris Tomer (Albany region rep. (518) 273-1851). *New York City, New York State, Great Britain, France, Canada, New Zealand.*

CITY LIGHTS LTD., P.O. Box 20355, Cherokee Station, New York, NY 10028; (212) 877-3235 or (212) 737-7049; Dee Staff and Davida Rosenblum. 9:00 A.M. to 5:00 P.M. Monday to Friday; 9:00 A.M. to 12:00 P.M. Saturday. Hosted and unhosted apartments from studios to four bedrooms in apartment houses and brownstones. Two night minimum stay. *Manhattan, Park Slope, Brooklyn Heights.*

NEW WORLD BED AND BREAKFAST, 150 Fifth Avenue, Suite 711, New York, NY 10011; (800) 443-3800; (212) 675-5600 (for calls from within New York state); Laura Tilden. 9:30 A.M. to 5 P.M. Monday to Friday. Hosted and unhosted apartments in high rises, brownstones, and carriage houses. Two night minimum stay. *Manhattan.*

NORTH COUNTRY BED & BREAKFAST RESERVATION SERVICE, Box 286, Lake Placid, NY 12946; (518) 523-3739; Lyn Witte. 11 A.M. to 8 P.M. daily. Private homes, country inns, and mountain resorts. *The Adirondack Mountains from Glens Falls north to the Canadian border, and from Lake Champlain west to Watertown.*

RAINBOW HOSPITALITY BED AND BREAKFAST, 9348 Hennepin Avenue, Niagara Falls, NY 14304; (716) 283-4794 or 754-8877; Marilyn Schoenherr and Gretchen Broderick. *Rochester, Niagara Falls, and Buffalo areas.*

URBAN VENTURES, INC., P.O. Box 426, New York, NY 10024; (212) 594-5650; Mary McAulay and Theresa Swink. *Manhattan and other boroughs.*

Pennsylvania

BED & BREAKFAST CENTER CITY, 1804 Pine Street, Philadelphia, PA 19103; (215) 735-1137; Jack Nespoli and Melody Ebner. *Philadelphia's Center City, Rittenhouse Square, Antique Row, Society Hill, University City, Art Museum area.*

HERSHEY BED & BREAKFAST RESERVATION SERVICE, P.O. Box 208, Hershey, PA 17033 (215) 533-2928; Renee Deutel. Call from 10 A.M. to 3 P.M. *Lebanon and Hershey.*

BED & BREAKFAST OF PHILADELPHIA, P.O. Box 680, Devon, PA 19333; (215) 688-1633; Sandra Fullerton, Carol Yarrow. *Philadelphia, its suburbs, and surrounding historic countryside, including Valley Forge, Chadds Ford, and New Hope.*

PITTSBURGH BED & BREAKFAST, 2190 Ben Franklin Drive, Pittsburgh, PA 15237; (412) 367-8080; Judy Antico.

BED & BREAKFAST OF SOUTHEAST PENNSYLVANIA, Box 278, R.D. 1, Barto, PA 19504; (215) 845-3526; Joyce Stevenson. Call anytime. Old farmhouses, restored grist mills, town and suburban houses. *Lehigh, Northampton, Berkshire, and Western Bucks counties.*

REST & REPAST BED & BREAKFAST SERVICE, P.O. Box 126, Pine Grove Mills, PA 16868; (814) 238-1484; Linda Feltman and Brent Peters. 7–11 P.M. Monday to Friday; noon to 6 P.M. Saturday. Farms, National Historic Register homes, apartments. *Penn State vicinity.*

Rhode Island

CASTLE KEEP, 44 Everett Street, Newport, RI 02840; (401) 846-0362; Audrey Grimes and Dorothy Ranhofer. 8 A.M. to 8 P.M. May to Sept. Restored colonials, Victorian mini-mansions, and condos by the sea. *Newport.*

GUEST HOUSE ASSOCIATION OF NEWPORT, P.O. Box 981, Newport, RI 02840; (401) 846-5444; Edwina Sebest, president of the Association.

Vermont

VERMONT BED & BREAKFAST, Box 139, Browns Trace, Jericho, VT 05465; (802) 899-2354; Sue and Dave Eaton. *Vermont only.*